THE
OSAGE

INDIANS OF NORTH AMERICA

THE
OSAGE

Terry P. Wilson
University of California at Berkeley

Frank W. Porter III
General Editor

CHELSEA HOUSE PUBLISHERS
New York   Philadelphia

On the cover Osage wearing blanket with ribbon appliqué trim

Editor-in-Chief Nancy Toff
Executive Editor Remmel T. Nunn
Managing Editor Karyn Gullen Browne
Copy Chief Juliann Barbato
Picture Editor Adrian G. Allen
Art Director Giannella Garrett
Manufacturing Manager Gerald Levine

Staff for THE OSAGE
Senior Editor Marjorie P. K. Weiser
Associate Editor Andrea E. Reynolds
Assistant Editor Karen Schimmel
Copy Editor Terrance Dolan
Deputy Copy Chief Ellen Scordato
Editorial Assistant Tara P. Deal
Senior Designer Laurie Jewell
Design Assistants Ghila Krajzman, Laura Lang
Associate Picture Editor Juliette Dickstein
Picture Research Ilene Cherna Bellovin
Production Coordinator Joseph Romano

5 7 9 8 6 4

Library of Congress Cataloging in Publication Data

Wilson, Terry P., 1941–
The Osage.

(Indians of North America)
Bibliography: p.
Includes index.
1. Osage Indians—History—Juvenile literature. 2. Osage
Indians—Cultural assimilation—Juvenile literature. 3. Indians
of North America—Great Plains-History—Juvenile literature.
4. Indians of North America—Great Plains—Cultural
assimilation—Juvenile literature. [1. Osage Indians. 2. Indians
of North America—Great Plains]
I. Title. II. Series
E99.O8W547 1988 978′.00497 87-34105

ISBN 1-55546-722-9
   0-7910-0365-5 (pbk.)

CONTENTS

INDIANS OF NORTH AMERICA

CHELSEA HOUSE PUBLISHERS

INDIANS OF NORTH AMERICA: CONFLICT AND SURVIVAL

Frank W. Porter III

The Indians survived our open intention of wiping them out, and since the tide turned they have even weathered our good intentions toward them, which can be much more deadly.

John Steinbeck
America and Americans

When Europeans first reached the North American continent, they found hundreds of tribes occupying a vast and rich country. The newcomers quickly recognized the wealth of natural resources. They were not, however, so quick or willing to recognize the spiritual, cultural, and intellectual riches of the people they called Indians.

The Indians of North America examines the problems that develop when people with different cultures come together. For American Indians, the consequences of their interaction with non-Indian people have been both productive and tragic. The Europeans believed they had "discovered" a "New World," but their religious bigotry, cultural bias, and materialistic world view kept them from appreciating and understanding the people who lived in it. All too often they attempted to change the way of life of the indigenous people. The Spanish conquistadores wanted the Indians as a source of labor. The Christian missionaries, many of whom were English, viewed them as potential converts. French traders and trappers used the Indians as a means to obtain pelts. As Francis Parkman, the 19th-century historian, stated, "Spanish civilization crushed the Indian; English civilization scorned and neglected him; French civilization embraced and cherished him."

Nearly 500 years later, many people think of American Indians as curious vestiges of a distant past, waging a futile war to survive in a Space Age society. Even today, our understanding of the history and culture of American Indians is too often derived from unsympathetic, culturally biased, and inaccurate reports. The American Indian, described and portrayed in thousands of movies, television programs, books, articles, and government studies, has either been raised to the status of the "noble savage" or disparaged as the "wild Indian" who resisted the westward expansion of the American frontier.

Where in this popular view are the real Indians, the human beings and communities whose ancestors can be traced back to ice-age hunters? Where are the creative and indomitable people whose sophisticated technologies used the natural resources to ensure their survival, whose military skill might even have prevented European settlement of North America if not for devastating epidemics and the disruption of the ecology? Where are the men and women who are today diligently struggling to assert their legal rights and express once again the value of their heritage?

The various Indian tribes of North America, like people everywhere, have a history that includes population expansion, adaptation to a range of regional environments, trade across wide networks, internal strife, and warfare. This was the reality. Europeans justified their conquests, however, by creating a mythical image of the New World and its native people. In this myth, the New World was a virgin land, waiting for the Europeans. The arrival of Christopher Columbus ended a timeless primitiveness for the original inhabitants.

Also part of this myth was the debate over the origins of the American Indians. Fantastic and diverse answers were proposed by the early explorers, missionaries, and settlers. Some thought that the Indians were descended from the Ten Lost Tribes of Israel, others that they were descended from inhabitants of the lost continent of Atlantis. One writer suggested that the Indians had reached North America in another Noah's ark.

A later myth, perpetrated by many historians, focused on the relentless persecution during the past five centuries until only a scattering of these "primitive" people remained to be herded onto reservations. This view fails to chronicle the overt and covert ways in which the Indians successfully coped with the intruders.

All of these myths presented one-sided interpretations that ignored the complexity of European and American events and policies. All left serious questions unanswered. What were the origins of the American Indians? Where did they come from? How and when did they get to the New World? What was their life—their culture—really like?

In the late 1800s, anthropologists and archaeologists in the Smithsonian Institution's newly created Bureau of American Ethnology in Washington, D. C., began to study scientifically the history and culture of the Indians of North America. They were motivated by an honest belief that the Indians were on the verge of extinction and that along with them would vanish their languages, religious beliefs, technology, myths, and legends. These men and women went out to visit, study, and record data from as many Indian communities as possible before this information was forever lost.

By this time there was a new myth in the national consciousness. American Indians existed as figures in the American past. They had performed a historical mission. They had challenged white settlers who trekked across the continent. Once conquered, however, they were supposed to accept graciously the way of life of their conquerors.

The reality again was different. American Indians resisted both actively and passively. They refused to lose their unique identity, to be assimilated into white society. Many whites viewed the Indians not only as members of a conquered nation but also as "inferior" and "unequal." The rights of the Indians could be expanded, contracted, or modified as the conquerors saw fit. In every generation, white society asked itself what to do with the American Indians. Their answers have resulted in the twists and turns of federal Indian policy.

There were two general approaches. One way was to raise the Indians to a "higher level" by "civilizing" them. Zealous missionaries considered it their Christian duty to elevate the Indian through conversion and scanty education. The other approach was to ignore the Indians until they disappeared under pressure from the ever-expanding white society. The myth of the "vanishing Indian" gave stronger support to the latter option, helping to justify the taking of the Indians' land.

Prior to the end of the 18th century, there was no national policy on Indians simply because the American nation had not yet come into existence. American Indians similarly did not possess a political or social unity with which to confront the various Europeans. They were not homogeneous. Rather, they were loosely formed bands and tribes, speaking nearly 300 languages and thousands of dialects. The collective identity felt by Indians today is a result of their common experiences of defeat and/or mistreatment at the hands of whites.

During the colonial period, the British crown did not have a coordinated policy toward the Indians of North America. Specific tribes (most notably the Iroquois and the Cherokee) became military and political pawns used by both the crown and the individual colonies. The success of the American Revolution brought no immediate change. When the United States acquired new territory from France and Mexico in the early 19th century, the federal government wanted to open this land to settlement by homesteaders. But the Indian tribes that lived on this land had signed treaties with European governments assuring their title to the land. Now the United States assumed legal responsibility for honoring these treaties.

At first, President Thomas Jefferson believed that the Louisiana Purchase contained sufficient land for both the Indians and the white population.

Within a generation, though, it became clear that the Indians would not be allowed to remain. In the 1830s the federal government began to coerce the eastern tribes to sign treaties agreeing to relinquish their ancestral land and move west of the Mississippi River. Whenever these negotiations failed, President Andrew Jackson used the military to remove the Indians. The southeastern tribes, promised food and transportation during their removal to the West, were instead forced to walk the "Trail of Tears." More than 4,000 men, women, and children died during this forced march. The "removal policy" was successful in opening the land to homesteaders, but it created enormous hardships for the Indians.

By 1871 most of the tribes in the United States had signed treaties ceding most or all of their ancestral land in exchange for reservations and welfare. The treaty terms were intended to bind both parties for all time. But in the General Allotment Act of 1887, the federal government changed its policy again. Now the goal was to make tribal members into individual landowners and farmers, encouraging their absorption into white society. This policy was advantageous to whites who were eager to acquire Indian land, but it proved disastrous for the Indians. One hundred thirty-eight million acres of reservation land were subdivided into tracts of 160, 80, or as little as 40 acres, and allotted to tribe members on an individual basis. Land owned in this way was said to have "trust status" and could not be sold. But the surplus land—all Indian land not allotted to individuals— was opened (for sale) to white settlers. Ultimately, more than 90 million acres of land were taken from the Indians by legal and illegal means.

The resulting loss of land was a catastrophe for the Indians. It was necessary to make it illegal for Indians to sell their land to non-Indians. The Indian Reorganization Act of 1934 officially ended the allotment period. Tribes that voted to accept the provisions of this act were reorganized, and an effort was made to purchase land within preexisting reservations to restore an adequate land base.

Ten years later, in 1944, federal Indian policy again shifted. Now the federal government wanted to get out of the "Indian business." In 1953 an act of Congress named specific tribes whose trust status was to be ended "at the earliest possible time." This new law enabled the United States to end unilaterally, whether the Indians wished it or not, the special status that protected the land in Indian tribal reservations. In the 1950s federal Indian policy was to transfer federal responsibility and jurisdiction to state governments, encourage the physical relocation of Indian peoples from reservations to urban areas, and hasten the termination, or extinction, of tribes.

Between 1954 and 1962 Congress passed specific laws authorizing the termination of more than 100 tribal groups. The stated purpose of the termination policy was to ensure the full and complete integration of Indians into American society. However, there is a less benign way to interpret this legislation. Even as termination was being discussed in Congress, 133 separate bills were introduced to permit the transfer of trust land ownership from Indians to non-Indians.

With the Johnson administration in the 1960s the federal government began to reject termination. In the 1970s yet another Indian policy emerged. Known as "self-determination," it favored keeping the protective role of the federal government while increasing tribal participation in, and control of, important areas of local government. In 1983 President Reagan, in a policy statement on Indian affairs, restated the unique "government to government" relationship of the United States with the Indians. However, federal programs since then have moved toward transferring Indian affairs to individual states, which have long desired to gain control of Indian land and resources.

As long as American Indians retain power, land, and resources that are coveted by the states and the federal government, there will continue to be a "clash of cultures," and the issues will be contested in the courts, Congress, the White House, and even in the international human rights community. To give all Americans a greater comprehension of the issues and conflicts involving American Indians today is a major goal of this series. These issues are not easily understood, nor can these conflicts be readily resolved. The study of North American Indian history and culture is a necessary and important step toward that comprehension. All Americans must learn the history of the relations between the Indians and the federal government, recognize the unique legal status of the Indians, and understand the heritage and cultures of the Indians of North America.

In 1834, the artist George Catlin traveled among the Osage, who were living along the Arkansas and Neosho rivers. At that time, the Osage were still wearing breech cloths, leggings, and moccasins made of animal skins, but blankets supplied by traders had replaced the traditional buffalo robes.

CHILDREN
OF THE
MIDDLE WATERS

Until the 1920s few non-Indian or Indian Americans knew or cared much about the Osage. Between 1919 and 1929, however, these people attracted national and international attention because of the money they received when oil was discovered on their land. Newspapers called them "the richest group of people in the world" and printed story after story about the reckless spending of the Osage, who built large houses but preferred to live in their traditional tipis and who bought expensive automobiles without knowing how to drive them. When the market for petroleum collapsed during the 1930s, the tribe's income was drastically reduced and the Osage's fame faded as rapidly as their money disappeared.

The history of the years before and after the period of oil wealth is similarly engrossing, telling of a rich tradition fervently kept by a proud and ancient people. Nearly 200 years before the discovery of oil on their reservation, the Osage lived in 5 permanent villages situated along tributaries of the Missouri River, which flowed through what is now the southwestern part of Missouri. But they had not always lived there. Tribal tradition recalls a migration from the east, forced by the numerous and powerful Iroquois Indians, who drove the Osage and other Siouan-language tribes, such as the Ponca, Kansa, Omaha, and Quapaw, from the banks of the Ohio River.

The Osage believed they were the children of the middle waters. The middle waters symbolized the universe of sky, earth, land, and water. Wah'Kon-Tah, the spiritual force of the Osage, ended the *ga-ni-tha*, or chaos, by separating the middle waters into the elements air, earth, and water. The Osage were divided into Sky People and Earth People. The Sky People, *Tzi-sho*, descended to this newly organized world from among the stars. They floated down, landing in a red oak tree. As they descended, their legs were stretched to grasp the limbs, and their arms were uplifted like the wings of an alighting golden eagle.

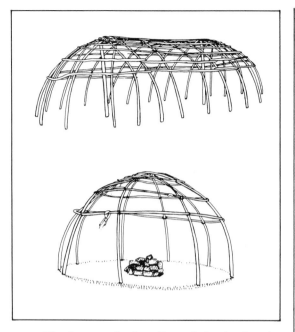

The framework of an Osage lodge (top) and sweathouse (bottom, used in purification ceremonies). Traditionally oval or circular in shape, the frames of Osage dwellings were constructed from hickory saplings.

These Tzi-sho found the *Hunkah*, Earth People, and joined them to make up the Osage tribe. The Osage traced their ancestry through their fathers and belonged to one of two divisions—the Sky People or the Earth People. The Sky People's 9 clans were symbolic of sky and peace, and the Earth People's 15 clans were symbolic of earth and war. These 24 clans were further divided into subclans, each with its own totem or sacred animal symbol: bear, buffalo, woodpecker, hawk, spider, and many others. Every clan chose leaders to sit on village and tribal councils, which handled most matters of government

and advised the two tribal chiefs, one from each of the two basic divisions. The tribal chief representing the Tzi-sho was responsible for matters of peace, and the one representing the Hunkah was responsible for matters of war. Tribal and village chieftainships were hereditary and passed from father to eldest son, or if the chief had no sons, to his eldest brother.

The Osage's permanent villages were arranged with great care. One wide dirt road went through each village, with smaller roads branching off at intervals. The two village chiefs lived on opposite sides of the main road in the center of the village. The clans of the Sky People lived on the same side as their chief and those of the Earth People on the side of theirs. In the village in which the two tribal chiefs lived, their households occupied the center position, with the homes of the village chiefs in a secondary position beside them. Individual extended families— mother, father, children, grandparents, and some dependent relatives—lived in circular or rectangular lodges made of hickory saplings. The bottoms of the saplings were stuck into the ground, and the tops were tied together. An interlacing of smaller saplings filled in the framework, which was covered with buffalo skins. Each lodge had an opening at the top for smoke to escape and a doorway on the eastern side so that persons emerging from it could chant prayers facing the rising sun. Although most lodges were much smaller, some were as much as 100 feet in length, 20 feet in width, and 10 feet in height. When the Osage went on their annual spring and autumn buffalo hunts they set up temporary camps of cone-shaped tipis for shelter.

Even though they had no written laws, Osage life was strictly regulated by tribal custom. Keepers and interpreters of tradition were chosen from the ranks of elder warriors known as the Little Old Men. These elders set standards of conduct for day-to-day living, directed the tribe's course of action in times of peace and war, and contemplated the nature of the universe. By attaching spiritual significance to all aspects of life, and by devising ceremonies—often very elaborate and lengthy rituals—to accompany everyday tasks and events, the Little Old Men ensured an orderly tribal existence.

The chiefs of the villages and the tribe almost always followed the Little Old Men's advice. If a leader proved ill suited to be chief, the tribal council could choose another to take his place. One of the most important functions of the chiefs was keeping the peace. Any warrior threatened by another could enter the Tzi-sho chief's lodge and claim sanctuary, which was never violated. The chiefs could spare the lives of Indians from other tribes who were captured by Osage warriors and could grant these captives membership in the tribe.

Chiefs also intervened in cases involving murder, considered by the Osage to be the most serious crime. Most murders resulted from fights, and the chiefs usually advised the relatives of the slain person to accept a peace gift

This Osage lodge, photographed in 1908, was covered with canvas instead of the usual buffalo hides but was otherwise similar to housing that had been used by the tribe for hundreds of years.

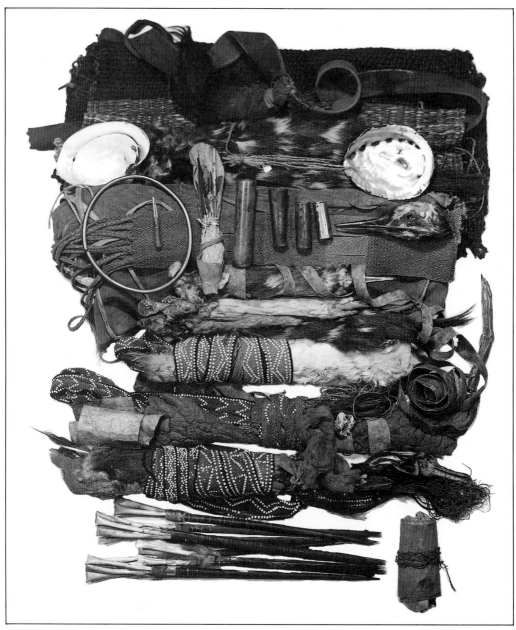

An Osage tattoo bundle containing instruments and other items used for tattooing. Among the contents of the buffalo-hair bag are the foot of a water bird, seven tattoo needles, feather brushes used to apply color, pouches made of weasel and skunk skins containing tobacco and medicine, brass tubes, a large brass ring, the head of a loon, a shell covered with heavy black pigment, and pieces of several human scalps.

in compensation. The heads of the two families involved would smoke the pipe of peace to seal the peace offering. The peace pipe symbolized a spirit of brotherhood, and those who smoked it together entered into a sacred bond of friendship. If the head of the injured family smoked the pipe and then later in a fit of anger killed the murderer anyway, the chief might order his death. If the murderer's relatives refused to pay the peace gifts to the murdered man's relatives, then the chief could force the family's village to pay it and expel the relatives from the tribe. This was a harsh punishment among people for whom group living was the only acceptable way of life.

Marriages between Osage were arranged. A young man's parents would choose his wife without his consent and often without his knowledge. If possible, a wife was selected from a different village, clan, and tribal division. The girl's relatives showed their decision to allow the marriage by accepting gifts offered by the boy's family; if the boy was unacceptable, the gifts were returned. Occasionally an Osage man might have more than one wife, usually the younger sister or sisters of the first one. A man would often marry his deceased brother's widow so that there would be a hunter to provide food for his nephews and nieces and protect their clan inheritance. Divorce was possible only if both husband and wife agreed. In such cases the husband was entitled to take back the gifts that had been given to his former in-laws at the time the marriage was arranged.

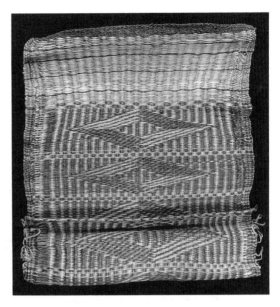

A bag woven from plant fibers, one of the containers in an Osage war bundle.

Osage men and women did different kinds of work. Men were responsible for protecting the villages and providing game for food. Women cared for young children, made the family clothing, built the tribe's dwellings, and prepared and cooked food. They were also the principal growers and gatherers of food, although the men often helped them lift and carry at harvest time. Men held exclusive political power until the 19th and 20th centuries, when Osage women, too, would participate in tribal politics.

The entire family, clan, and village were responsible for child rearing. Osage men taught the boys the skills needed for hunting and warfare, and women taught the girls domestic skills and how to grow crops and gather other foods. Children were introduced to the

An Osage woman and child of the early 1800s from the McKenney-Hall Portrait Gallery of American Indians. *The woman wears non-Indian clothing.*

beliefs and morals of the tribe through stories their grandmothers told them. Every Osage child was constantly instructed, usually by example and almost never by physical punishment, in the tribe's customs. Those slow to learn or heed the lessons were first teased and shamed into obedience and then ignored and ostracized if unacceptable behavior persisted. Being shut off from one's family and clan was very serious; there was nothing to take the place of playing together, sharing meals, and participating in other communal activities.

Non-Indians who saw them considered Osage men and women particu-larly handsome. The 19th-century American writer Washington Irving, who encountered many tribes during his travels throughout the country, described them as "the finest looking Indians in the West." Many Osage were exceptionally tall; it was not uncommon for the men to be well over six feet. Osage men wore their hair roached: They shaved their head, including their eyebrows, leaving only a scalp lock of hair about two inches high and three inches wide running from the forehead to the back of the neck. They wore loincloths, leggings, and moccasins, all made of deerskin, and bearskin or buffalo robes. They pierced their ears to accommodate numerous ornaments and wore bracelets on their wrists and forearms. Prominent warriors tattooed their chest and arms. For many ceremonial occasions Osage men painted designs on their face, arms, and legs with natural dyes. Younger warriors might strut about, showing off to attract the attention of the young women; however, mature warriors and older men held themselves erect, moving gracefully and slowly, with a dignity befitting their age and station.

Osage women had long hair that hung loosely down their back. They wore deerskin dresses, moccasins, and leggings. The dresses were cinched at the waist with wide belts of woven buffalo-calf's hair. When brightly colored wool became available through European traders, they fashioned their belts from this material. The women adorned themselves with earrings and bracelets and tattooed their body, often more elaborately than the men. Mature, married women walked with the same impressive dignity as the older men. Osage women perfumed their garments with chewed columbine seed and powdered their body with a dark substance derived from a beanlike flowering plant. They applied the dried pulp of pumpkin to their face to improve their complexion. At puberty the girls were separated from all men except members of their immediate family. They were closely guarded by the tribe's older women, who carried knives to enforce proper conduct by the men toward their charges.

The cluster of neat Osage villages along the rivers in the Mississippi Valley were filled with a well-regulated society of warriors and women, who remained content for generations before the coming of the Europeans. Life was not without hard work, but it was simple, following the familiar cycles of nature, attuned to animals, plants, and the seasons. In all areas of life they acknowledged the presence of Wah'Kon-Tah, the spiritual originator of the Osage universe. Their rituals celebrated this presence and helped perpetuate the myths of the tribe. One ritual, the dance of creation, reenacted the Sky People's descent to earth. Dancers wore

Le Soldat du Chêne, The Soldier of the Oak, received his name after using an oak tree as shelter to fight off several enemies. He wears the traditional roached hairstyle of Osage warriors.

buckskin leggings trimmed with fringe that represented eagle feathers. They kept time with ceremonial gourd rattles that, when shaken, imitated the rattling of the acorns dislodged from the oak tree that had received the Sky People.

It was a delicately balanced world into which the non-Indians would intrude, changing forever the lives of the children of the middle waters. ▲

Three Osage warriors (left to right), Mun-ne-pus-kee (He-Who-Is-Not-Afraid), Ko-a-tunk-a (The Big Crow), and Nah-com-ee-shee (Man of The Bed) dressed in the typical style of young Osage men.

THE
COMING
OF
EUROPEANS

In June 1673 Father Jacques Marquette and Louis Jolliet navigated the Wisconsin River down from New France (Canada) to the Mississippi River, hoping they could follow it west to the Pacific. Instead, they were disappointed to find that it flowed southwest into territory already claimed by their colonial rivals, the Spanish. Nonetheless, the explorers claimed all the land of the Mississippi Valley for the king of France and proclaimed all its inhabitants subjects of the Crown.

A few years later two other French explorers, whose names are unknown, paddled canoes up the Missouri River to the Osage River, both tributaries of the Mississippi. The first Indian village they came upon was inhabited by the Little Osage. The Frenchmen wrote the villagers' name as *Ouazhigi*, after hearing neighboring Indians call them *Wah-Sha-She*. (The name was later written in English as Osage.) The two French explorers eventually found four more vil-

lages that were home to another major branch of the tribe known collectively as the Great, or Grand, Osage.

The Osage women and children pretended to be indifferent to the strangers, while the men stood apart scowling, waiting to see if these men were enemies. When the newcomers appeared to pose no immediate threat, the tribespeople moved near to examine them closely. The Indians stared at the white men's pale skin and marveled at their beards, bushy eyebrows, and chest hair. They called the French and later European visitors *I'n-Shta-Heh*, Heavy Eyebrows. From these people who prized clean-shaven heads, this slang term expressed an attitude close to contempt.

The Mississippi Valley's chief attraction for the Europeans was its abundant supply of fur-bearing animals. French traders pushed south of the Great Lakes to exploit many varieties of pelts and selected the Osage as busi-

An artist's impression of Father Jacques Marquette discovering the Mississippi River.

ness partners. They encouraged the tribe to raid the nearby Caddo, Pawnee, and Padouca (Comanche) tribes for their stocks of furs as well as another important trading commodity, slaves. Like other Indian tribes, the Osage had always captured some members of enemy tribes. Many of these Indian slaves learned Osage customs and were incorporated into the tribe. With the coming of the French, who eagerly acquired Indians captured by the Osage for shipment and sale to rich plantation owners in the West Indies, the taking of slaves increased. In return for furs and slaves, the French gave the Osage mirrors, woolen blankets, metal tools, alcohol, guns, and horses.

The French believed they had chosen their allies well. The tribe occupied a strategic position on the Missouri River that made it possible to keep others from exploring or from using the entire river system for commercial or military purposes. Waterways were the only cheap and easy transportation through the wilderness, so the French gladly provided the Osage with the flintlock muskets and the horses they demanded in exchange for unimpeded use of the river. With these goods the Osage were able to dominate other tribes. Repeated military success and the development of a strong desire for European trade items caused the Osage to become ever more aggressive in relations with their Indian neighbors and extremely arrogant toward everyone, including their French allies.

The area west and south of the Osage eventually drew the interest of the French, not only for its furs but also for its Indian population. The French viewed the Indians as potential allies in the struggle to curb possible Spanish settlement. Fur companies dispatched *voyageurs* (explorers or guides) and *coureurs de bois* (fur trappers and traders) on trading expeditions to other tribes. The Osage, sure of their own power and determined to keep enemy warriors from obtaining guns, attacked French expeditions on several occasions. They seized muskets and am-

munition from traders who had not yet reached their destination and furs from those returning home. Outraged French protests were met with bland denials by the Osage, who realized that the incidents would be overlooked and written off as being necessary to keep the tribe's goodwill intact. The Osage viewed the French policy as a sign of weakness and were only further emboldened by it.

In 1723 the French king sent Etienne Veniard, Sieur de Bourgmont, to establish alliances with other tribes and hold the Osage in check. He was an excellent choice for the difficult task. Eleven years earlier, as commandant of Fort Detroit, Bourgmont had welcomed a

Voyageurs traded furs and hides at French settlements such as this one along the Mississippi River.

party of Osage warriors who came to aid the French garrison when it was besieged by hostile tribes. Bourgmont was so impressed with these tall, fearsome fighters that he went with them to their homes after Fort Detroit was saved. He lived among the Osage and the Missouria tribes for three years, and fathered a son by a woman of the latter tribe. The Indians respected and liked Bourgmont. He was taller than most French men and possessed an outgoing personality. He had left only when summoned to France to receive a royal decoration for his defense of the frontier.

When Bourgmont returned to North America in 1723, his first act was to supervise the construction of Fort Orleans. That summer he organized and led an expedition of 64 Osage and 100 Missouria west to the territory of the Kansa tribe. When several of the French, including Bourgmont, fell ill from a fever, the Osage took it as a bad sign and abandoned the adventure to begin their fall buffalo hunt. Neither their absence nor his illness kept Bourgmont from carrying out his mission. He negotiated an alliance of the Padouca, Missouria, Kansa, Oto, and Osage that called for them to live in peace and friendship and paved the way for further French expansion.

Hoping to cement the newly peaceful relations and further bind the Indians to his home country, Bourgmont invited several chiefs to accompany him to France. Although a number of leaders from the Osage and other tribes traveled as far as New Orleans, only one from each tribe actually sailed to Europe. The group arrived in Paris in September 1725 and stayed several months, attracting much attention. They were frequently guests at the country estates of the French nobility, where, dressed in their traditional costumes, they performed dances and demonstrated their hunting skills. Upon returning home, the chiefs enthusiastically described the wonders they had seen.

French interest in the Mississippi Valley diminished between 1724 and 1733. Fort Orleans was abandoned after several years, leaving the French in the region without the protection of a fortified garrison. In 1729 reports of an Osage attack in which 11 members of a fur-trapping party were killed alarmed French authorities. Investigation revealed that only a single independent French trapper traveling with Indians of another tribe had been murdered. The Osage conveyed their apologies through the Missouria, explaining that they had believed the man to be an Indian and insisting that they wished no harm to any of the French. This explanation was accepted, and the occasional killings of other voyageurs in future years were always followed by similar Osage apologies. By reluctantly accepting these apologies, the French acknowledged the weakness of their presence on the Missouri.

Osage and Kansa warriors continued to attack voyageurs and coureurs de bois in the 1730s and 1740s in an effort to keep them from bringing fire-arms to the Comanche and other Plains tribes. Several tribes joined these hostile actions, possibly encouraged by English agents from the east, who hoped to weaken the French hold on western territory. Despite the numerous attacks on their traders, French officials were determined to maintain their alliances with the Osage and other Indians in the Mississippi Valley. They feared the growth of English influence throughout the region, brought on by the cheaper and superior trade goods sent from the English colonies to the north and east.

In 1755 the French called on the Osage to help repel the forces led by the English major general Edward Braddock, who was marching against Fort Duquesne, located at the forks of

At the battle of Fort Duquesne in 1755, French forces, aided by Indian warriors, routed the English troops and killed their leader, Major General Edward Braddock.

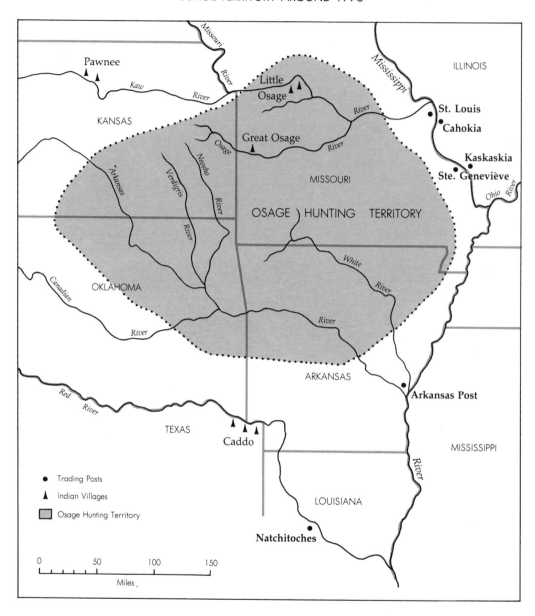

the Ohio River (now the city of Pitts-
burgh). As many as 200 Osage warriors
joined those of other French-allied
tribes to ambush Braddock's troops of
British regulars and the colonial militia
led by a young colonel, George Washington. The Indians, waiting in ambush
behind trees and rocks along the troops'
route, picked off their red-coated ad-
versaries, including Braddock himself,
with ease. Washington was wounded,
but escaped. An Osage oral tradition

tells of one tribal chief who, bored with this style of fighting, leaped from behind his cover and began singing and dancing his contempt for the enemy. The English fired on him, one of the few attackers they could see, and felled the courageous warrior.

The French were victorious at Fort Duquesne, but they made little use of the Osage in their struggles with the English for control of colonial America, known as the French and Indian Wars. The English, with a much larger colonial population in North America and command of the sea, defeated France. The Treaty of Paris, signed in 1763, gave to Spain, England's ally, the area west of the Mississippi River that included the tribe's villages. Like the rest of France's Indian allies, the Osage were never directly informed about the peace treaty.

Soon after the war's end, French from farther east appeared in numbers among the tribes of the Mississippi Valley, preferring to live under Spanish rule rather than in former French territory that had been ceded to England. The Spanish had reluctantly accepted the territory, called Louisiana, which stretched to the Gulf of Mexico. They needed a buffer between themselves and the populous and rapidly expanding English colonies but did not desire additional land and Indians to add to their administrative burden. Not until 1768 did Spain finally assume formal authority over governmental functions in Louisiana, and even then the French often transmitted official policy.

In 1770 the Spanish lieutenant governor, Antonio de Ulloa, arrived in St. Louis to take command of Upper Louisiana and carry out orders from the governor general in New Orleans. He made it clear that the Osage tribe was to cease its incessant warfare with neighboring Indians and reside peaceably under Spanish guidance. The Osage ignored his orders and continued to raid their traditional enemies.

Part of the problem of Osage hostility lay in the nature of Spain's Indian policy in Louisiana. In other Spanish territories Roman Catholic priests had converted many Indians to Catholicism, and the religion's theology of peace among humankind was thought to have curbed outbreaks of violence. The priests' influence was bolstered by small but permanent military posts. However, stretched to the limit economically and politically at the time they acquired Louisiana, the Spanish adopted the French way of dealing with the tribes through licensed traders. When a problem erupted, they attempted to control troublesome Indians such as the Osage by withholding trade goods.

This policy had flaws. Merchants in St. Louis were willing to forgive Osage attacks on their Indian neighbors—and even raids on non-Indians—because of the tremendous profits they earned on the furs they received from the tribe. Also, the Osage committed their crimes in the Arkansas and Natchitoches trading districts, away from officials in St. Louis. In 1790 the Spanish governor in

Auguste Chouteau, the fur trader who for eight years controlled trade with the Osage.

New Orleans, Hector Baron de Carondelet, did impose a sanction prohibiting all trade, but two years later, irritated at its failure, he declared war on the Osage. After several minor skirmishes, the Osage raided a Spanish settlement, Ste. Geneviève, in 1794, killing several traveling traders.

Auguste Chouteau, a cofounder and leading citizen of St. Louis, proposed a solution to Governor Carondelet's problem with the Osage. Since 1764 Chouteau had moved among the Osage, trading extensively and establishing good relations with them. He now offered to build a fort near the tribe to show Spanish authority in exchange for a six-year monopoly of Osage trade.

Chouteau got the monopoly and built Fort Carondelet in 1795. For several years the post was a center of profitable trade for him and his brother Pierre, a reliable source of trade items for the Osage, and a symbol of Osage alliance with the Spanish. The Osage warriors did not stop raiding their enemies but at Auguste Chouteau's urging they pursued their activities in the north, away from the Spanish settlements.

As a reward for their success, Carondelet in 1800 extended the Chouteaus' monopoly for another four years. An ambitious Spanish fur trader, Manuel Lisa, complained of favoritism and gathered names of other St. Louis merchants on a petition. This protest against the extension of the Chouteaus' monopoly resulted in a lengthy legal battle. The monopoly was granted to Lisa in 1802. By then, however, the Chouteaus had figured out a way to maintain their advantage and leave their Spanish competitor a much less profitable trade than he expected. They had persuaded a large band of the Osage to move their permanent villages to another location, away from the territory covered by Lisa's monopoly.

In the last decades of the 18th century the Osage fared well. Using their strategic location on the Missouri and Osage rivers and access to European trade goods to their advantage, they dominated the surrounding tribes, who feared the Osage's superior weapons and military potential. This prosperity led to rapid growth in the tribe's size—the number of Osage warriors increased from about 800 in the 1770s to nearly 1,500 by 1800—which may have made a break in the unity of the tribe almost inevitable.

Osage warriors followed various clan and tribal leaders on extended forays to hunt buffalo or raid enemies. The hold of the hereditary chiefs, the Hunkah and Tzi-sho, as well as that of the Little Old Men, weakened as clan chieftains led independent expeditions of warriors, seeking individual glory and fame. One frequent resting place was in what is now Oklahoma, a campsite where the Verdigris and Neosho rivers flow into the larger Arkansas River. This area, later known as Three Forks, offered good spring water, a warm climate, and excellent navigation down the Arkansas to the Mississippi and eventually to New Orleans. In particular, access to New Orleans convinced the Chouteaus to set up a new trading post there.

The move initiated by the Chouteau brothers in 1802 was opposed by the two tribal chiefs. Ironically, one of them, Pawhuska, or White Hair, had been made chief years earlier with the connivance of the Chouteaus. They had supported Pawhuska in displacing Claremore (also known as Clermont), a legitimate heir to tribal chieftainship, who was then a young boy. Unable to budge Pawhuska, Pierre Chouteau found a minor clan chieftain, Cashesegra, or Big Foot (known among the Osage as Makes-Tracks-Far-Away), who agreed to move to Three Forks. Chouteau urged the Osage to follow Cashesegra. About half of the Great Osage decided to relocate, not so much because of Cashesegra or Chouteau, but because of the influence of Claremore. He was indisputably the real leader of the Osage who moved to the new village at Three Forks, which became known as Claremore's Town. The chief was called Town Maker by admiring fellow Osage.

The separation of Claremore's followers into a distinct Arkansas band took place 125 years after the coming of the Europeans. Over those years the lives of the Osage had changed steadily as the tribe increasingly reacted to the activities of the newcomers. The Osage were still absorbing the shock of the geographic and political split manipulated by the Chouteaus in 1802, when events in Europe led to new changes that would be even more drastic for the tribespeople than any they had experienced before. ▲

Clermont, son of Claremore the Town Maker, was primary chief of the tribe in 1834. As signs of his authority, he holds his war club and his leggings are trimmed with scalp-locks, tufts of hair attached to pieces of scalp, taken in warfare from his enemies' heads.

RESERVATION
LIFE

Napoleon Bonaparte, the ambitious ruler of France, wanted to reclaim Louisiana from Spain. Because Louisiana was the least profitable section of Spain's vast and expensive American colonial empire, the Spanish agreed to cede the territory back to France. News of the transfer alarmed United States president Thomas Jefferson. He believed that a French-held Louisiana would be a greater threat to the westward expansion of his nation than the weaker Spanish colony.

Jefferson sent emissaries to Napoleon in 1803 to suggest shared control of the Mississippi River and the city of New Orleans. They were surprised when the French ruler offered to sell them the entire Louisiana Territory for $15 million, an offer that was quickly accepted. Napoleon needed money to finance his European wars, and as a result, the huge expanse of largely unexplored land, which included the territory in which the Osage and many other Indians lived, changed hands once again.

Soon after the Louisiana Purchase, eastern Indian tribes displaced by non-Indian settlers began moving into Osage territory. These newcomers, pressured by the U.S. government to move to less crowded locations west of their traditional lands, included the Cherokee, Choctaw, Creek, and Chickasaw. When they arrived, they joined the Osage's traditional enemies, such as the Potawatomi and the Sac and Fox, in threatening the tribe's security.

Claremore's band mounted raid after raid against the encroaching tribes. Irritated, the federal government instructed Pierre Chouteau, newly appointed Indian agent for Upper Louisiana, to curb the Osage's hostility. Chouteau attempted to reduce Claremore's influence by reuniting the Osage under Pawhuska. His plan failed, however, as Claremore's dynamic leadership attracted more and more young warriors from the Missouri bands.

Chouteau then decided to use gifts of trade goods and threats of cutting off further trade to force the Osage to give

A copy of the 1803 treaty in which France sold the Louisiana Territory to the United States. When the document was signed it was not known exactly how much land was involved, but the final boundaries of the Louisiana Purchase doubled the size of the United States.

up some of their land. In 1808 he convinced the tribal chiefs to sign a disadvantageous treaty with the U.S. government, ceding an area about 200 square miles in what is now southern Missouri and northern Arkansas for only $7,500 in cash and trade goods. During the next few years thousands of Cherokee and non-Indians moved onto this land, leading the Osage and other tribes to suspect that the crowding would result in demands for further land cessions.

Their suspicions proved accurate. In November 1815 the federal government asked the Osage to sell some territory north of the Arkansas River, on both sides of the present Oklahoma-Arkansas border. Even Claremore agreed to the terms of the purchase, made three years later. His village had been attacked by a war party of emigrant Indians while the band's warriors were away on their fall buffalo hunt. More than 80 women, children, and old men were killed and 100 more carried off. When the warriors returned home, they retaliated against the marauders, and the captives were rescued. In the process, however, many warriors were killed, leaving Claremore's fighting strength drastically reduced.

The Osage soon discovered that the two previous land cessions were not

OSAGE LAND CESSIONS BETWEEN 1808 AND 1825

NEBRASKA

ILLINOIS

KANSAS

Missouri

Osage

River

River

MISSOURI

Neosho River

Verdigris River

OKLAHOMA

Canadian

Claremore's Band

Missouri Bands

River

Red

ARKANSAS

Arkansas River

River

TEXAS

River

LAND CESSIONS

Treaty of 1808

Treaty of 1818

Treaty of 1825 -

Osage Reservation 1825

LOUISIANA

0   50   100
Miles

enough to satisfy the land-hungry new-comers. In 1822 Auguste and Pierre Chouteau convinced some of the Missouri bands to abandon their old villages and move farther west to a site on the Neosho River near modern Salina, Oklahoma, where a large trading post operated by the Chouteaus could supply their needs. Three years later those Osage still living in Missouri agreed to give up claims to all their remaining land in what is now the states of Missouri, Arkansas, Oklahoma, and Kansas. All that was left was a reservation in the southern part of present-day Kansas that would be set aside for the tribe by the U.S. government. Claremore's band, and the Missouri bands that had moved in 1822, did not relocate to the reservation at this time, but they would later.

The reservation was 50 miles wide and 125 miles long. Its southern border corresponded to the modern boundary between Kansas and Oklahoma. The U.S. treaty commissioners assured the Osage that several square miles of "neutral lands" would be maintained east of the reservation as an unoccupied buffer zone between the tribe and the advancing frontier. In the late 1820s and the 1830s the Osage were largely left alone and continued to live as they always had. Gradually, however, the neutral lands were violated by non-Indian settlers who then trespassed on the reservation.

Hunting and warfare continued to be the major occupations of Osage men. The ongoing struggles against encroachment by the emigrant Indians from the east, along with the traditional enmity of various western Plains tribes, forced the Osage to place greater importance on war-making leadership. Through warfare young men could become warriors, so there was always enthusiasm for battle. The war-mourning ceremony, a ritual for slain fighters, also contributed to the pattern of constant conflict. The entire tribe would grieve for four days, at the end of which the men, their faces painted black with white and yellow markings, would complete the ceremony by taking an enemy scalp.

Before relocating to the reservation, Osage women had raised pumpkins, corn, beans, and squash and had supplemented their diet by gathering nuts, wild potatoes, persimmons, berries, prickly pear cactus, and milkweed sprouts from the surrounding forests. They also collected various herbs, leaves, and bark, which were used for seasoning and preserving foods. As the forests filled with emigrant Indians and settlers, the Osage obtained less of their food by growing and gathering and came to rely more on the buffalo as their main source of food, often trading the hides for those items they had formerly grown or gathered themselves.

A buffalo hunt required as much planning as a military action. The hunters, who were on horseback, often set controlled fires to drive the buffalo toward a river where other hunters waited in ambush. Sometimes they built surrounds—corrals constructed of logs and brush—and drove the animals into them to be killed. The slaughtered buffalo were given to the women, who accompanied the men to the temporary hunting camps, to butcher and prepare. The women built miniature lodges over fire pits and laid slabs of meat over the lodges' wooden framework to smoke. Once cooked, some of the meat was cut up and mixed with tallow (animal fat) and stored in parfleches—storage bags made of buckskin. The remainder was cut into thin strips and jerked—dried in the sun—to preserve it.

The Osage's existence was precarious, subject to nature's whims. Prolonged hot dry spells, exceptionally harsh winters, or scarcity of the various animals they hunted could make life uncomfortable and interfere with the food supply. But the Osage's lives were not solely devoted to food getting; there were diversions. Entire villages, adults and youngsters alike, participated in games. Balls made from buffalo hide stuffed with buffalo hair were used in a sport similar to field hockey that was played, separately, by both men and women. Men and women together played the moccasin game. The players sat in two rows, and four moccasins, lined up side by side, were placed between them. A small object was placed in one moccasin. While chanting to a beaten drum, one side would manipulate the moccasins in the hope of confusing the other side, which had to guess what moccasin the object was in. The Osage frequently wagered their most precious belongings—buffalo robes, horses, lariats (ropes used to catch or tether livestock), bridles, tanned skins, and jewelry—on the outcome of these games. Their livelihood was so precarious as it was that the Osage thought little of gambling away their belongings, many of which could be easily replaced from their surroundings. Sometimes they played for days, at times losing all their possessions. No

Indians used every part of the buffalo: the meat for food, the skins for clothing and shelter, the hair for making textiles, the bones for tools and jewelry, and the sinew for thread.

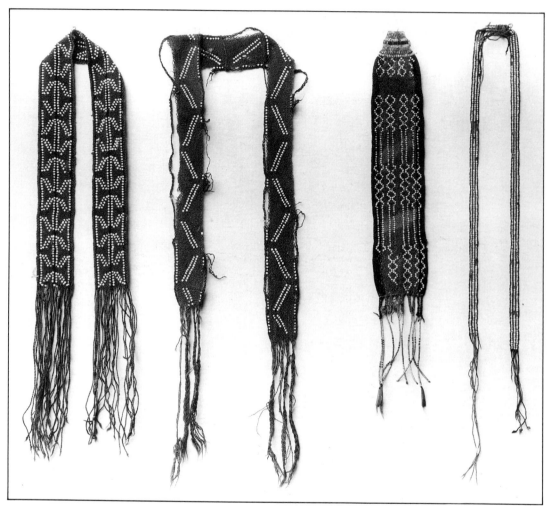

Belts and a garter (second from right) woven from buffalo hair.

one scolded the losers; only complainers were scorned.

During the 1840s the Osage increased their trade in buffalo hides and began trading mules and horses as well. In 1847 they received on credit $24,000 worth of goods. They then traded the goods to the Comanche for 1,500 mules, which they traded back to the original creditors for nearly $60,000 worth of goods, their shrewd business instincts netting them a profit of $36,000 in merchandise.

The Osage supplied the Comanche and Kiowa with guns, powder, lead, cloth, blankets, and other manufactured items in return for buffalo robes, mules, and horses. The livestock traded to the Osage had been stolen by the Comanche and Kiowa from ranches in Texas and Mexico. Sometimes these marauders captured the ranchers' children as well and traded them to the Osage, who turned them over to government authorities, gaining goodwill for the tribe. Occasionally young Osage warriors accompanied the Comanche on their raids along the Santa Fe Trail. The two tribes maintained their profitable trade until 1853 when the Comanche began receiving manufactured goods from the United States as a condition of a treaty they had signed. Throughout the 1850s the Osage continued to hunt buffalo themselves and traded as many as 20,000 robes annually.

The U.S. government's goal was to "civilize" the Indians by teaching them non-Indian religious values and turning them into farmers. Protestant missionaries had been active among the Osage in the Missouri Territory since the early 1800s, and in the Kansas Territory, Catholic missionaries prevailed. Efforts to convince the tribe to take up farming failed because hunting was so productive. A government treaty of 1839 promised them cattle, hogs, plows, and axes along with the services of a blacksmith, a miller, and instructors in agriculture. The few Osage who did want to become farmers were discouraged by their chiefs and prominent warriors, who believed that if their men became farmers, the tribe would abandon its traditional way of life. Those who accepted the government's livestock were frequently condemned by fellow tribespeople and often prematurely slaughtered the animals to keep the peace. Livestock given to the chiefs usually was traded for goods or served at elaborate feasts. When principal chief George White Hair and 12 families prepared to farm by plowing and fencing land in 1842, the other leaders threatened to replace him with a more conservative chief. The following year White Hair slaughtered his livestock for a grand party and forgot about farming.

Ironically, the government's policy toward Indians on reservations almost ensured the continuation of Osage resistance. The authorities feared that the money and supplies issued annually to the tribes, called annuities, might be used to purchase liquor, the increasing consumption of which was becoming a problem among Indians. The government dispensed the annuities to the village chiefs, instead of directly to heads of families as the tribespeople wanted. The chiefs in turn distributed them to the people in the bands. This gave them considerable economic control; anyone who did not agree with a chief risked being cut off financially as well as socially.

The Osage, like other Indians, were pressured to wear non-Indian clothing. Most of the eastern emigrant Indians had earlier adopted the non-Indian's boots, trousers, shirts, and hats adorned with feathers. Osage men preferred their leggings, breech cloths, and moccasins to the confining collars and boots of the Heavy Eyebrows, whose body odors, they said, could not escape and made them smell bad. Those who dared to put on the clothing of the newcomers were ridiculed by traditional Osage, who scorned most non-Indians except members of the military and some traders.

Missionaries were slightly more successful than the government at persuading the Osage to change. In 1847 Father John Schoenmakers arrived with a Jesuit contingent to establish a mission on the Neosho River near what is now St. Paul, Kansas. That same year another Catholic order, the Sisters of Loreto, opened a convent school for girls to complement Father Schoenmakers's school for boys. Both schools gave instruction in agriculture and manual skills, such as carpentry and cooking, as well as reading, writing, and other academic subjects. The missionaries were able to persuade the majority of mixed-bloods—Osage with a non-Indian ancestor or ancestors—to practice some agriculture. Many mixed-bloods converted to Catholicism at the urging of their non-Indian fathers, most of whom were French traders and wanted their children to become Christians. However, Osage full-bloods, tribespeople with Indian ancestors only, rarely converted and continued to shun farming as a way of life.

Neither the Jesuits nor anyone else could influence the Osage to give up drinking liquor, and by the late 1840s alcoholism was a significant problem. The reservation agent reported in 1848 that a third of the 1,500 horses the

Osage acquired from the Comanche were traded to peddlers for whiskey. Having had no experience with liquor before the arrival of the Europeans, many Osage drank until they became intoxicated and then sought more liquor when sober.

During the 1850s settlers trespassing on the reservation caused trouble. The "neutral lands" that had been set aside in 1825, as a buffer zone at the eastern edge of the reservation, and land assigned to other tribes north of the Osage, were opened to non-Indians for settlement in 1854. Hundreds of settlers ignored reservation boundaries and set up farms on Osage land. In 1859 the agent from the Indian Office assigned to administer the government's programs among the Osage called in federal troops to remove some of the squatters. However, many trespassers were overlooked and many of those ejected came back after the army withdrew. As the best land in the Kansas Territory was taken, would-be settlers pressed for the abolition of the reservation and the opening of its land to non-Indian farmers.

Pressure for reservation land eased in 1861 when the Civil War began. American Indians, including the Osage, were drawn into the nation's struggle. The reservations of the Cherokee, Choctaw, Chickasaw, Creek, and Seminole, known collectively as the Five Civilized Tribes, bordered that of the Osage on the south. The Five Civilized Tribes had originally come from Southern states, and many of their members owned black slaves. Although some of these tribes' members favored the Union, the majority supported the Confederacy. All five contributed warriors to the Confederate army and elected delegates to the Confederate congress. The Osage's involvement in the war resulted solely from personal loyalties. They had encountered few black men, whom they called *nika-sabe*, and they had no understanding of the issues dividing the nation.

Shortly after the war began in April 1861, the Osage agent left for Washington, D.C. In July and August John Mathews, a Confederate sympathizer and trader who lived among the Osage, led forces of pro-Southern whites and Osage warriors in several skirmishes against civilians sympathetic to the Union cause. Father Schoenmakers, a strong Union man, was forced to flee his mission on the Osage reservation. The mission, situated between Mathews's Confederate forces and Union army encampments, became the site of considerable military action. In September Lieutenant Colonel James G. Blunt and the Sixth Kansas Cavalry defeated Mathews's company, routing it completely. Mathews was killed in the battle, and his death left the Confederate cause in southeastern Kansas without a leader.

Homesteaders rush to claim former Indian land after being signaled that it was open for settlement.

The Confederacy sent Albert Pike, the superintendent of Indian agencies for the Confederacy and a persuasive orator, to form the Osage and other tribes into an alliance. Pike induced the Five Civilized Tribes and many Plains tribes as well to sign treaties with the Confederate government. On October 2, 1861, 57 Osage chiefs and councillors also signed a treaty. Only Four Lodges, Little Bear, and Striking Axe, all leaders of the Little Osage, refused to sign the agreement. The Confederacy promised to protect the tribe against enemies and assured them that their reservation would never be included within the boundaries of any state or territory. In exchange the Osage would allow the Confederacy to establish a military post on the reservation and would furnish at least 500 warriors for the Confederate army.

But on the Osage reservation, there was no Confederate military leadership. Discouraged by this and by the proximity of Union forces throughout the war, most Osage did not remain loyal to the Confederacy. Only the bands led by Black Dog and Big Chief continued to support the Confederate cause. During the war these bands fled to Creek and Cherokee country, where they stayed until Union forces invaded those reservations, at which time they returned to Kansas.

Meanwhile, Chief Little Bear, who had not signed the Confederate treaty, enlisted with some of his Little Osage in a Union force, the Ninth Kansas Infantry. These were the only Osage who actually donned uniforms and attempted to become American-style soldiers. Very few persisted; most found even the relatively loose discipline, restrictions, and drills of a frontier unit too confining for their independent warrior attitude. Four Lodges (Chetopa), another Little Osage who had not signed the treaty, raised a contingent of 200 warriors that became part of the Second Regiment of the Union's Indian Brigade. However, they deserted when the force marched south to confront the Confederate tribes in Indian Territory.

In May 1863, 22 Confederate officers disguised as civilians crossed the Osage reservation on a secret mission to rally several Plains tribes to action against the Union. They were discovered by 10 Osage who questioned them about their business. The Confederates claimed they were Union soldiers, but the Osage insisted on taking the officers to the Union post at Fort Humboldt, located on the reservation, to verify their identity. The Confederates tried to escape, shooting a warrior who attempted to stop them. The Indians took their dead comrade and raced to their village to tell the story.

The Osage chiefs Hard Rope and Little Beaver set off with about 200 warriors in pursuit of the Confederate officers. When they overtook the soldiers, the Osage split into several groups, herding the Confederates toward an area where the Verdigris River ran swift and deep, cutting off an escape. During the chase, one Osage warrior and two Confederate officers were killed. Cor-

Osage band chiefs (left to right): Striking Axe, Four Lodges, Paw-ne-no-pashe, Big Chief, and Hard Rope.

nered on a sandbar and out of ammunition, the soldiers dismounted and faced the Indians in hand-to-hand combat. Eighteen were scalped and beheaded and two escaped. Finding that one of the dead was bald, the Osage warriors removed his long beard and added it to the scalps they carried off.

For the Osage it was a great victory. Many warriors had *counted coup*, touched enemy soldiers to prove their bravery and prowess in combat. The next day the warriors led Union soldiers to the scene of the battle and watched them bury the casualties. The Osage buried their own dead in the traditional manner, painting the faces of the corpses and placing them in a seated position in shallow graves covered with mounds of rocks. After they feasted with the Osage and watched their scalp dance, the Union soldiers informed the warriors that they could keep the horses, saddles, pistols, rifles, and sabers of the slain Confederates.

Local Union supporters and government officials applauded the Osage's minor contribution to the Union cause, but their gratitude proved short-lived. Even before this incident—as early as 1862—there had been talk of the tribe ceding its land for non-Indian settle-

An Osage warrior holds a bow and arrow in his left hand and a coup stick in his right. The warrior who touched his enemy with a coup stick achieved the highest of war honors.

ment. It was not the Osage's objection to giving up their land that had stopped the government at the time, but the practical problem of where to relocate the tribe. When the war ended in 1865, the United States compelled the Five Civilized Tribes to sign new, punitive treaties because of their support of the Confederacy. Among the treaty concessions forced upon them was one stipulating that other "friendly Indians" would be relocated onto the western parts of their reservations in Indian Territory.

Federal officials also negotiated a new treaty with the Osage. The tribe gave up a 30- by 50-mile area of the eastern part of the reservation, along with a 20-mile-wide strip from the northern part of their lands. The ceded territory quickly filled with settlers who displaced the Osage and soon pushed onto remaining reservation land as well. Government attempts to eject the squatters from Osage land were ineffective.

At about this time, hostilities broke out between the Osage and some Plains Indians. The Cheyenne were angry because the Osage were acting as scouts for Lieutenant Colonel George Armstrong Custer and other military commanders who were campaigning against them. In 1868 the Osage, fearing Cheyenne revenge, refused to go on their spring buffalo hunt. This left them short of food for the winter.

The rapidly growing non-Indian population in the region continued to press for the entire Osage reservation to be opened for settlement. One typical letter from a settler to his representative in Congress stated that the Osage were "lazy, dirty vagabonds" who should not be allowed to possess "land so fair and rich as this. We want this land to make homes. Let us have it." The settlers neither knew nor cared that the tribe had already lost its original home in Missouri and had been promised the Kansas reserve to live on "as long as the grass grows and water flows." A commissioner from Washington, D.C., visited the reservation in 1869 and reported that the tribe was harassed by the Plains Indians and sur-

This traditional Osage grave, marked by a mound of rocks and an upside-down American flag, was photographed in Indian Territory around 1870.

rounding non-Indian settlers, more than 2,000 of whom were illegally squatting on Osage land. Some of these trespassers had taken over the Osage's cabins and fields while the Indians were away hunting, and they constantly stole horses from the tribal pony herds.

A team of government surveyors assesses the Osage's land in 1866 in preparation for settlement by non-Indians. Although the Osage were promised title to the reservation in Kansas "as long as the grass grows and water flows," the tribe was forced to move onto new land in Indian Territory in 1871.

That same year a new agent, Isaac T. Gibson, arrived. He was a Quaker, a member of the peace-loving Society of Friends, many of whom were chosen by President Ulysses S. Grant as Indian agents in the hope that they would provide honest administration in a sympathetic manner. Gibson quickly gained the confidence of the desperate Osage. The Quakers were pacifists, and Gibson convinced the tribe that their best course was to move south into Indian Territory rather than to fight for their land in Kansas.

Some of the leaders, especially Hard Rope and Four Lodges, considered trying to oust the intruders by force. But they joined the majority in attending a council to discuss removal. The meeting had been scheduled for August 1870, but it was delayed until September so the Osage could hunt buffalo. After two days of debate, the chiefs and councillors reluctantly accepted a treaty whereby the Osage would move to new land to be purchased from the Cherokee with money they had received from the 1865 treaty. At that time, the Kansas reservation would be sold to settlers for $1.25 an acre.

One leader, Joseph Paw-ne-no-pashe (Not-Afraid-of-Longhairs), lived up to his name by demanding certain guarantees: that the Osage would be allowed to hunt buffalo outside the new reservation, that the new reserve would be protected from trespassers, and that the land would be owned communally by the tribe and not be allotted to individuals for farming, as was happening on other tribes' reservations. Paw-ne-no-pashe's efforts were in vain: The buffalo herds disappeared in 1875, intruders were a continuous problem on the new reserve, and in 1906 the government divided the reservation into individual holdings.

Once they agreed to a reservation existence the Osage accepted a degree of governmental control that greatly restricted their traditional life-style. At one time the major power in their region, the Osage now saw their position erode as non-Indians settled around and finally among them. Anxious to postpone the inevitable destruction of their way of life, they clung to traditional beliefs as much as possible. Because of their determination to remain independent, the Osage were among the last of the Indians in Kansas to lose their land. Their spirit and stubbornness would help make them the last tribe to surrender its reserve in Indian Territory, as that area became the territory, later the state, of Oklahoma. ▲

Osage agent Isaac Gibson (standing), the first Quaker to be appointed to the position, with Chief Four Lodges (left) and a mixed-blood interpreter.

In 1836, George Catlin painted Wah-chee-te, the wife of Chief Clermont, with her child. She was dressed in non-Indian clothing, unusual at that time among the Osage, who rejected the influence of the non-Indians.

A NEW HOME
IN
INDIAN TERRITORY

The Osage were not pleased about the move to a new reservation. According to one newspaper account, on the day after the removal treaty was signed in 1870 "the air was filled with the cries of the old people, especially the women, who lamented over the graves of their children, which they were about to leave forever." Most of them left their Kansas homes in the late fall for the semiannual buffalo hunt and returned to the new reserve in northeastern Indian Territory in the early part of 1871. A few, however, did not settle there until 1874.

The 96th meridian marked the eastern edge of the new reservation, and the Arkansas River, a rough diagonal from northwest to southeast, was the western boundary. The Osage had purchased 1,470,559 acres from the Cherokee. They gave their linguistic cousins, the Kansa tribe, about 102,400 acres in the northwestern corner of the reserve. The Kansa's land was separated from the Osage reservation and incorporated into present-day Kay County when Oklahoma became a state in 1907.

Those Osage who moved to Indian Territory in 1871 were fairly content with their new surroundings. The eastern half of the reservation was thickly wooded with oak and hickory trees that gradually thinned into tangled scrub oak known locally as blackjack. Streams, rock-ribbed hills, and several open meadows broke up the acres of forest. Farther west the tall, thick grass of the rolling prairie ended at the high bluffs and timbered banks of the Arkansas River. An abundance of game— deer, turkey, quail, beaver, otter, raccoon, coyote, and timber wolf—thrived in the tall grass and woodlands. Just west of the Arkansas River, buffalo could be found. Only the Cheyenne and Arapaho, recently located on a reserve south and west of the Osage, competed with them in hunting for buffalo. The Cherokee to the east did not want any contact with the "uncivilized" Osage, and the Creek tribe was too far south to be a threat.

Agent Isaac Gibson believed that the Osage were capable of learning to survive in the non-Indian world. He en-

47

Augustus Captain (second from left), a mixed-blood Osage, attempted to remain on his land in Kansas after the Osage were relocated to Indian Territory, but he was forced to rejoin the tribe. With him are (left to right) Black Dog, Joseph Paw-ne-no-pashe, and John N. Florer, a trader.

thusiastically described them as "richly endowed by nature, physically and morally." Comparing them to the troublesome Kansas settlers who continued to hunt, cut timber, and run cattle on Osage land, Gibson wondered "which of these people are the savages?" However much he admired the Osage's sense of communal welfare, Gibson was obligated to carry out the U.S. government's policy toward the Indians, which instructed him to change them into God-fearing, English-speaking, patriotic farmers.

Gibson hired five non-Indian farmers and several farmhands to open agricultural stations for the various bands. Oxen, plows, wagons, and farm implements were brought in to prepare the hard prairie ground for cultivation. Because Indian ponies were not sturdy enough to pull plows, the farmers used oxen to brake the sod. During the winter of 1872–73, when the rest of the tribe left to hunt buffalo, 57 men stayed behind and were paid to cut and split 81,000 rails for fencing the plowed fields. Every Osage family that fenced at least five acres of farmland was encouraged to build permanent housing and offered help in doing so.

Between 1873 and 1875 fruit orchards were planted, wells dug, and more than 200 homes built. Every family that agreed to live in a house received tables and chairs, brooms and washboards, cups and saucers, knives and forks. Near the agent's residence, on a hill overlooking the site that would become the city of Pawhuska, the government had built a sawmill, a gristmill, a commissary, a physician's office, a church, a gun shop, barns, smithies,

harness shops, and wagon shops. Four private traders' stores offered the Osage the material goods of Anglo-American civilization.

In addition, Gibson had hired a religious-minded staff, many of them ministers, deacons, and lay members from a variety of Protestant denominations, to reinforce the activities of Quaker missionaries active in the area. "The moral tone at the agency," Gibson boasted, "will compare favorably with the most refined neighbors in the states."

However, even though some Osage men were used to helping their wives tend small fields in forest clearings, they did not want to become full-time farmers. They wanted to remain hunters and warriors: That was to be an Osage. Then, between 1870 and 1875, the buffalo herds disappeared at the

A pen-and-ink drawing of Main Street, Pawhuska, in 1874.

Non-Indians hunting buffalo for profit and sport rapidly and severely reduced the once populous herds. The disappearance of these animals deprived the Indians of their main source of food.

hands of non-Indian hunters who slaughtered them for their hides and for sport. The near extinction of the Indians' main source of food contributed to widespread hunger among all tribes living in the area. Some Osage turned to Gibson for aid. A few did try farming, only to become discouraged and quit when a prolonged drought and grasshopper invasions from the north destroyed their crops in 1873 and 1874.

Nevertheless, some Osage who took up farming became successful at it. In 1875, reservation farms produced 50,000 bushels of corn, 20,000 bushels of wheat, and a sizable vegetable crop. Nearly all the reservation's cultivated acreage recorded that year belonged to mixed-bloods and intermarried citizens—non-Indian men accepted into tribal life because of marriage to Osage women—or to full-blood Little Osage

power to refuse the tribe's requests for their money.

During the 1880s the Osage prospered under their constitutional government. The majority of families were able to avoid farming and manual labor because the quarterly cash annuities payments allowed them to buy most of the supplies they needed. The payments had increased in the late 1870s when the tribe leased some of its lush pastures and abundant creek water to Texas cattle herders wishing to fatten their herds before crossing the state line to railroad depots in Kansas. With Miles negotiating on behalf of the tribe, more than 350,000 acres were leased under multiyear contracts.

In the 1890s the Osage and other tribes came under considerable pressure from various groups in Washing-ton, D.C., to divide their reservations into individual allotments. The United States wanted to make the Oklahoma and Indian territories into the state of Oklahoma, but before it could, all land had to be individually owned. Through the exceptionally hot summer of 1893, representatives from Washington met with the Osage in Pawhuska, the Osage capital, to discuss allotment. The five-member committee appointed to meet with the commission, which included James Bigheart and his son Peter, refused to consider individual land ownership, pointing out that the tribal constitution forbade it. Although the representatives could not convince the committee to accept allotment, they did persuade them to open the meetings to all members of the tribe. By the time the commission left several weeks later,

A delegation of Osage representatives that traveled to Washington, D.C., in the early 1890s to negotiate land leases.

The town of Pawhuska in the early 1880s. Agency Hill can be seen in the background.

nearly all the mixed-bloods and some full-bloods favored allotment in principle.

One major objection among those Osage opposed to allotment was that many non-Indians were fraudulently included on the tribal roll—the official list of members. A government investigation found only 25 illegal names on the roll. This did not satisfy the antiallotment group, which had claimed that more than 500 people were fraudulently listed. (Investigations almost a century later would prove that the protesters were correct: Many intermarried non-Indians and mixed-bloods who had only long-distant Indian ancestry were enrolled fraudulently. This could not have been proven at the time because of ill-kept records and a fire in 1893 that destroyed the National Council building that contained family documents.

But evidence from nontribal sources unavailable at the time confirmed the Osage's claims.)

In 1894 Osage agent H.B. Freeman estimated that between 1,000 and 5,000 non-Indians lived on the reservation. Non-Indian men who had married Osage women had accompanied the tribe on the move from Kansas. They soon had been joined by merchants, cattle herders, clergy, and agency workers. By 1904 the non-Indian population had expanded to between 10,000 and 15,000, far outnumbering the 2,200 Osage.

In 1906 nearly 2,000 people lived in Pawhuska, and other towns—Hominy, Foraker, Big Heart, and Fairfax—were growing. Drugstores, harness shops, meat markets, and banks lined the streets, and doctors, lawyers, and contractors had established offices as well.

The reservation was crossed by three railroad lines, and several small telephone companies provided a link between communities.

Although efforts to teach the Indians to farm and accept Christianity had made little progress, officials in Washington still hoped for long-range change. The education of Indian children would prepare them for the end of reservation existence. The children would be placed in boarding schools to separate them from tribal life. They would learn to speak English, praise God and the United States of America, lead regulated lives, and perform manual and domestic labor as training for farm life.

The boarding schools, located both on the reservation and off, were run in military fashion. Students donned uniforms, marched to and from classes, drilled regularly, and were subject to fairly rigid discipline. School days were highly structured from the time the children arose at 5:45 in the morning to the playing of taps at 8:30 each evening. For half of the day, Monday through Saturday, each child was assigned work detail—household chores for the girls, farm or craft work for the boys. The remainder of every day was spent in classes and drills. Two brief recesses were the only playtime the children were allowed.

The Osage were among the most vocal of the tribes protesting the boarding-school regime. They disliked having their children removed from home and made to perform non-Indian work. As a result of the parents' objections, the agency hired extra help to do the chores usually assigned to students at similar schools. The cost per student of running the agency school therefore ranked highest of the 164 schools in the federal system.

Nearly all the parents objected as well to the lengthy separations from their children. Often parents visiting the schools decided to take their sons and daughters home. Some, such as full-blood Frank Corndropper, bypassed the agency altogether and complained directly to the commissioner of Indian affairs: "I have two small boys," he wrote. "They are penned up in the school and they don't like it, they get lonesome and homesick and it affects their health; I ask your permission to take them from school Friday evening and return them Sunday evening." Corndropper did not get permission to take his sons home, but eventually the mixed-bloods, because of their greater ties to the non-Indian culture, were allowed to have their children on weekends; full-bloods were not.

Osage children who attended boarding schools off the reservation were regarded as especially troublesome because they did not respond to discipline and were not as easily intimidated as children from other tribes. Whereas tribes on other reservations depended heavily on government annuities to support themselves, the Osage came to rely less and less on this kind of aid. Instead, they received quarterly interest payments on the money from the sale of the Kansas reservation as well as the fees for leasing grazing land and cutting timber on the eastern half of the reserve. With no economic threat to back up their authority except the very drastic one of withholding annuities—which would be certain to lead to serious confrontation—agents and school superintendents had little control over the Osage children.

The U.S. government, fearful that an autonomous Osage National Council would become too powerful, abolished the tribe's constitutional government on April 1, 1900. In its place, a council of 15 Osage men was set up to conduct tribal affairs, under the direct supervision of the commissioner of Indian affairs. The end of the tribe's constitutional government, however, did not end Osage resistance to the government's civilization program and allotment plans. Indeed, if it had been merely a question of governmental pressure, the tribe might very well have held out indefinitely. According to a law passed in 1889, no tribe could lose its communal ownership of a reservation unless its members agreed to such a proposal.

Osage students stand in front of the girls' dormitory at the agency boarding school in Pawhuska. The Osage were one of the most outspoken tribes in protesting the boarding-school regime, which attempted to eliminate Indian culture through military-style regimentation and forced separation of children from their parents.

An Indian camp near the agency in Pawhuska, photographed in the early 1900s. By the beginning of the 20th century, few Osage were still following their traditional way of life.

The Osage were the last Indians in either Indian Territory or Oklahoma Territory—areas joined as the state of Oklahoma in 1907—to give up their reservation. The final decision in 1906 to give up communal ownership owed as much to population and cultural pressures as to federal Indian policy. By then the number of people of pure Osage descent had dwindled to 838, and the number of mixed-blood tribal members had climbed to 1,156. Some full-blood families still lived in lodges and followed their traditional life-style, but the Osage territory was no longer a haven of Indian culture, secure against the changing outside world. Like the Indians on neighboring reservations, the Osage had to walk a narrowing path between rejection and partial acceptance of the non-Indian culture. They emerged transformed, retaining many pieces of cultural baggage, losing or discarding others, and accepting some new ones.

Between 1871 and 1906 the Osage became a minority on their own land and were constantly subjected to the government's attempts to civilize them. Faced with the allotment to individuals of their communally owned reservation land, they realized that resistance would only delay, but not altogether avoid, the loss of their land and life-style. Although the Osage finally accepted the idea of full allotment in 1906, it was fortunate that they did resist: An unexpected economic development that had occurred 12 years earlier would enable them to retain a degree of control over their resources that less stubborn tribes were unable to exercise.▲

The band chief Tchong-tas-sab-bee (The Black Dog), was the second most influential leader of the tribe. Blind in his left eye, he stood almost seven feet tall and was the largest man in the Osage nation.

THE
RICHEST PEOPLE
IN THE
WORLD

In 1894 the Osage's healthy finances were boosted in a way that would affect every aspect of the tribe's future: Oil was discovered on the reservation. Henry Foster, a successful oil speculator, had asked the Bureau of Indian Affairs, the U.S. government agency within the Department of the Interior that was responsible for protecting the interests of the Indians, to grant him exclusive rights to explore for and extract oil and natural gas on the Osage reservation. Recent discoveries of petroleum in Kansas had led him to believe that oil would also be found just south of the border in Osage territory. The Bureau granted Foster's request and in mid-March 1896 the Osage National Council accepted his lease. He was to pay the tribe a royalty of 10 percent on all sales of petroleum produced from reservation wells and $50 annually for each gas-producing well.

By 1904 there were 155 oil-producing wells and 18 gas wells on the reservation. A pipeline connected the reservation wells to a Standard Oil refinery at Neodesha, Kansas. Foster's lease was to expire in 1906, but well in advance Congress voted to extend it. The new terms doubled the royalty rate on gas wells, gave the Interior Department the right to set the oil royalty, and limited Foster's exclusive claim to the eastern half of the reservation, where his wells were located.

The publicity surrounding the presence of oil led to intense local interest in how the reservation would be allotted. By 1906 the majority of tribespeople agreed in principle to individual land ownership, and the National Council decided to allow allotment of the reservation. On June 28, 1906, Congress passed the Osage Allotment Act. It was rumored that some of the fullbloods on the Osage allotment delegation could almost recite the act from memory, especially the part that concerned the tribal roll, so great was their concern that it benefit only Osage. The act stated that all persons enrolled as

Oil gushes from a well in northeastern Osage County.

Osage before January 1, 1906, and all born between then and July 1, 1907, would share in the division of the land and resources. Because tribal membership was matrilineal, based on descent traced through female ancestors, children born to Osage women and non-Indian men, but not children born to Osage men and non-Indian women, would be included on the tribal roll.

The Osage Allotment Act contained a particularly significant stipulation that was unique among the mineral-rich Oklahoma tribes. All subsurface minerals were to belong communally to the entire tribe rather than to individuals beneath whose parcels of land the minerals were found. Instead of allowing chance to decide which persons would get rich from oil and gas royalties, the tribespeople would share equally in the wealth from the reservation's underground resources.

There was great tension among parents expecting children in the months before July 1, 1907. Potential mineral riches and the desirability of their land made inclusion on the roll highly valuable. One baby was taken in the fifth month of pregnancy by Caesarean section, a risky operation at the time, so that it could be included on the 1907 roll. The baby defied the attending physician's prediction of a short life and lived a normal span of years, collecting a share of the tribe's income. One Osage couple expected the birth of their child near the July 1 deadline. When the woman went into labor, her husband saddled his horse and nervously paced the front porch of his house. As soon as he heard his newborn's cry, he galloped to Pawhuska to record the birth at the agency. There he realized that he did not know whether the baby was a boy or a girl. Embarrassed, the flustered father gambled and filed a girl's name. He guessed wrong, and so a male allottee with a decidedly female name was listed on the roll.

When the Osage tribal roll was closed in 1907, it contained the names of 2,229 persons: 926 full-bloods and 1,303 mixed-bloods, including Indian and non-Indian adoptees. No minimum degree of relationship, or blood quantum, had been established for inclusion on the list. Non-Indians could legally inherit an allottee's share. The shares, commonly referred to as headrights, could be divided among heirs and further subdivided as they passed from generation to generation. Inheritance could also cause an individual to own more than one headright or several plots of land.

Osage children born after the roll was closed were recognized as members of the tribe, but they did not share in the tribe's income. In time two

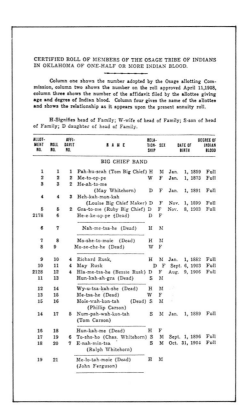

CERTIFIED ROLL OF MEMBERS OF THE OSAGE TRIBE OF INDIANS IN OKLAHOMA OF ONE-HALF OR MORE INDIAN BLOOD.

Column one shows the number adopted by the Osage allotting Commission, column two shows the number on the roll approved April 11,1908, column three shows the number of the affidavit filed by the allottee giving age and degree of Indian blood. Column four gives the name of the allottee and shows the relationship as it appears upon the present annuity roll.

H-Signifies head of Family; W-wife of head of Family; S-son of head of Family; D daughter of head of Family.

ALLOT-MENT NO.	ROLL NO.	AFFI-DAVIT NO.	NAME	RELA-TION-SHIP	SEX	DATE OF BIRTH	DEGREE OF INDIAN BLOOD
			BIG CHIEF BAND				
1	1	1	Pah-hu-scah (Tom Big Chief)	H	M	Jan. 1, 1859	Full
2	2	2	Me-to-op-pe	W	F	Jan. 1, 1873	Full
3	3	2	He-ah-to-me				
			(May Whitehorn)	D	F	Jan. 1, 1891	Full
4	4	3	Heh-kah-mon-kah				
			(Louise Big Chief Maker)	D	F	Nov. 1, 1899	Full
5	5	2	Gra-to-me (Ruby Big Chief)	D	F	Nov. 8, 1903	Full
2178	6		He-e-ke-op-pe (Dead)	D	F		
6	7		Nah-me-tsa-he (Dead)	H	M		
7	8		Mo-she-to-moie (Dead)	H	M		
8	9		Mo-se-che-he (Dead)	W	F		
9	10	4	Richard Rusk,	H	M	Jan. 1, 1882	Full
10	11		May Rusk	D	F	Sept. 6, 1903	Full
2128	12	4	Hla-me-tsa-he (Bessie Rusk)	D	F	Aug. 9, 1906	Full
11	13		Hun-kah-ah-gra (Dead)	S	M		
12	14		Wy-u-tsa-kah-she (Dead)	H	M		
13	15		Me-tsa-me (Dead)	W	F		
15	16		Moie-wah-kon-tah (Dead)	S	M		
			(Phillip Carson)				
14	17	5	Num-pah-wah-kon-tah	S	M	Jan. 1, 1889	Full
			(Tom Carson)				
16	18		Hun-kah-me (Dead)	H	F		
17	19	6	To-sho-ho (Chas. Whitehorn)	S	M	Sept. 1, 1896	Full
18	20	7	E-nah-min-tsa	S	M	Oct. 31, 1904	Full
			(Ralph Whitehorn)				
19	21		Me-lo-tah-moie (Dead)	H	M		
			(John Ferguson)				

A list of Osage on the tribal roll

classes of Osage emerged: the haves, allottees who received full shares until their deaths, and the have-nots, who received money only if they inherited full or partial headrights from relatives.

In 1916 J. George Wright, the superintendent (the title replaced *agent* in 1908) of the Osage agency, advertised for an auctioneer to auction off the tribe's mineral leases to oil companies. The Interior Department would pay the person $10 a day with money from Osage tribal funds. Colonel Walters ("Colonel" was his given name), an experienced hand at land and livestock sales, was the successful applicant. Walters, whose usual fees were $50 to $100 an auction, took the job for its publicity value. A decade later he would wear proof of the wisdom of that decision—a diamond-studded badge valued at $3,000, a large diamond ring, and a jewelled tiepin worth $500. The badge and ring were gifts from the Osage in appreciation for his auction of the mineral leases that made them rich. The tiepin was a gift from the Miller brothers, owners of the nearby 101 Ranch, who also benefited from the regional development of oil and gas resources.

Walters presided over the lease auctions under the "million dollar elm" on Agency Hill. Wooden bleachers were built for bidders and spectators. In bad weather, the auctions were held in the Kihekah Theater in downtown Pawhuska. Representatives from all the major oil companies with headquarters in Tulsa, Oklahoma, attended. Owners of highly successful companies, such as Bill Skelly, E. W. Marland, Frank Phil-

(continued on page 73)

The "million dollar elm," under which auctions of the Osage's mineral leases were held in good weather. The house of the Osage Indian agent is in the background.

ARTISTS WITH RIBBON AND YARN

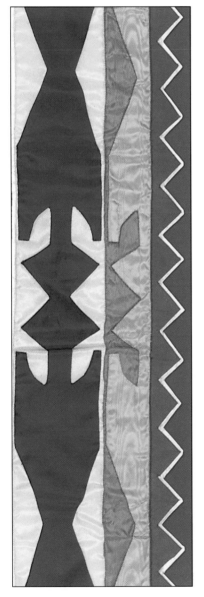

Long ago the Osage made clothing of deerskin and other prepared hides, trimmed with dyed porcupine quills. Sashes and other accessories were made by braiding twisted strands of plant fibers, buffalo hair, and coyote and rabbit fur.

After European traders arrived with colored cloth, yarn, and beads, Osage women became artists working with the new materials. Steel scissors and needles, fine thread, and, later, sewing machines gave them new techniques for making and decorating clothing. Broadcloth, a woven wool fabric, and silk and satin ribbons replaced deerskin with quill decoration. Commercially dyed yarn was easier for fingers to weave than animal and plant fibers.

The Osage women adapted the new materials to their traditional clothing styles. They sewed design shapes cut out of cloth onto a cloth background, a technique known as appliqué. They were particularly skilled in reverse appliqué, designs cut into layers of ribbon so that the contrasting color of the bottom layer can be seen.

Osage people today usually wear the same kind of clothing as other Americans, but on special occasions they put on these spectacularly decorated traditional garments. The garments made by Osage artists in the last century are treasured by museums and art collectors as well as by tribal members.

Detail of ribbon border for a red wearing blanket. Reverse appliqué of blue reveals the underlying yellow, of green shows the underlying pink. The triangular edge is appliquéd to the background.

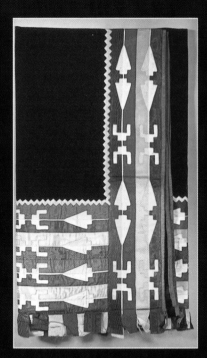

*Elaborate silk ribbon appliqué
and reverse appliqué on a red
wearing blanket, which would
have been made for the first-
born child in an Osage family.*

*A black wool wearing blanket
folded to show the machine-
stitched silk ribbon trim. Each
design strip consists of three
layers of ribbon in four rows,
alternately blue and pink over
purple and red, and white over
green.*

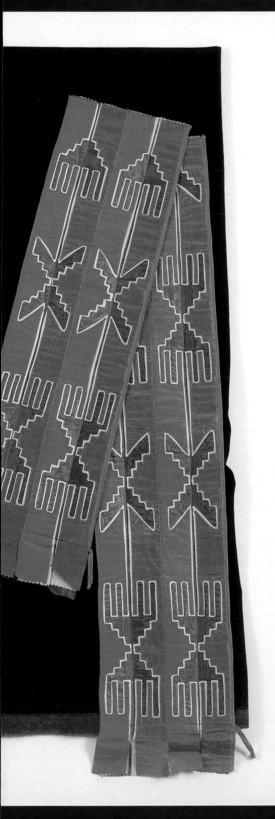

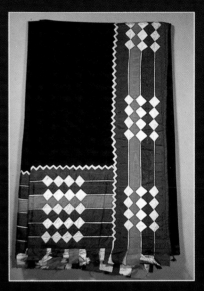

The white and ivory underlying ribbons on this blanket form a traditional "beaver tail" design.

Woman's dance robe, made and used as a skirt in the late 19th century.

Front (above) and back (opposite page, top) of a man's vest. The designs on the front are formed by small metal disks; the designs on the back and across the bottom are of loom-woven bead strips.

Red shirt trimmed with white beads.

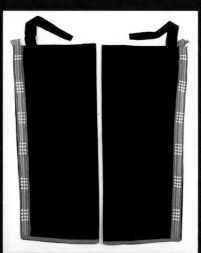

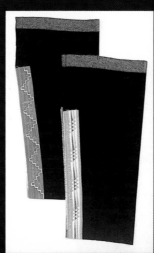

Far left: *Man's leggings, part of a dance costume, with ribbon trim in "beaver tail" design.*
Left: *Woman's leggings trimmed in two different ribbon appliqué designs, one on the inside and the other on the outside, edged with white beads.*

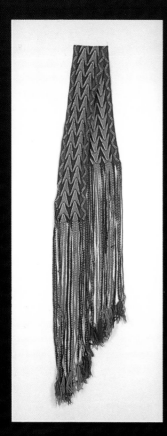

A 45½-inch long sash of colored wool yarn and white beads in double arrow design.

Finger-woven sash of yarn in "lightning and arrow" design, 39 inches long and 4¼ inches wide. The 25-inch-long fringe has white beads braided in with the yarn.

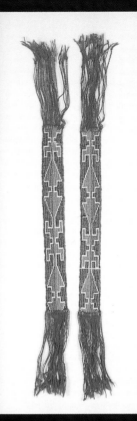

A pair of garters, made of colored beads woven on a loom and fringed with wool.

Finger-woven wool sash in chevron design, with white beads on braided fringe.

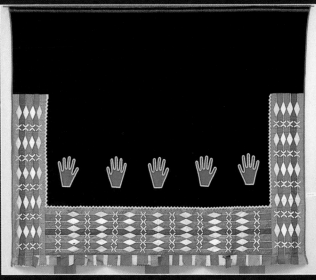

Above: *Wearing blanket of broadcloth trimmed with satin ribbon and beads, made in 1981 by Kimberly Ponca Stock of Fairfax, Oklahoma. After selling it to a collector, she borrowed it for the Miss Indian America contest, saying "I've got wearing rights to it."* **Left:** *A wearing blanket made half a century earlier has the same hand design, which signifies friendship.*

Oil tycoon Frank Phillips (front row, second from right), whose purchases of mineral leases enhanced the Osage's wealth, wears a Plains Indian–style war bonnet given to him by the tribespeople. The traditional Osage headdress was a beaver bandeau such as that worn by Osage council member and band chief Bacon Rind (front row, second from left).

(continued from page 64)

lips, G. F. Getty, and his son J. Paul Getty, attended frequently. Next to them sat "wildcatters," independent drillers short on capital but optimistic that cheap tracts in untried areas might yield lucrative wells.

The west side of the reservation proved to be one of the richest oil fields in American history. By 1928 Walters had auctioned off leases worth $157 million to eager drillers, who sometimes paid more than $1 million for the right to explore on a single 160-acre lot. Once, when the bidding opened at $100,000 and dropped to $25,000 increments only after the $1 million mark was reached, one bidder raised a bid of $1.3 million by only $1,000. "Oh, that stuff won't get us anywhere!" Walters scoffed disdainfully.

Walters could identify buyers' signals, bids indicated with barely perceptible hand or head motions. W. J. Knupp, an independent driller, was known as a "bargain counter," a person who seldom bought a lease for more than the starting minimum bid. On one hot, stuffy auction day, Knupp dozed off and awoke to find that the auctioneer had interpreted his sleepy nodding as a $300 winning minimum bid. Walters gleefully refused to accept Knupp's explanation, and the sale was made. Within a year Knupp realized every wildcatter's dream: The tract had five producing wells, and he sold the lease for nearly a million dollars.

Lucky transactions like this were rare. Oil companies paid geologic surveyors thousands of dollars to identify likely tracts and spent millions to purchase lots adjacent to already-producing leases. Yet information and capital did not guarantee fortune. One firm paid $1 million for a lease that was virtually surrounded by pumping wells and spent an additional $450,000 drilling, only to find one "duster," or dry hole, after another.

For the most part, Osage allottees were content to stand on the sidelines, watching others compete for leases and accepting the growing payments. Royalties peaked in 1925, when the annual income from each headright reached $13,200. The average size of an Osage family during the 1920s was 5; therefore, if all of a family's members were included on the allotment roll, the total family income for 1925 would have been $66,000, exceptional wealth in an era of minimal income taxes and low prices. In contrast, their hardworking superintendent earned only $3,000 annually, and that was considered a well-paying job. The Osage rarely used their royalty checks to pay for ordinary living expenses; income derived from leasing their allotted surface land to non-Indian farmers and ranchers usually provided them with the necessities of life.

Many Osage entered wholeheartedly into the world of conspicuous consumption. In the 1920s their spending sprees delighted both newspaper writers and readers. Government workers and missionaries, however, feared that the Osage would learn unwanted lessons of excess and extravagance. Their fears were especially well founded when it came to buying automobiles. It was commonly said that in rural Osage County there were more Pierce Arrows (a leading luxury car) than in any other county in the United States. The Osage coveted automobiles even though most could not drive them. They gladly hired chauffeurs to guide their expensive cars along the county's dirt roads.

Most Osage preferred to lease acreage to non-Indians who farmed and ranched instead of farming themselves, but several were interested in livestock and owned expensive herds. However, these animals were strictly for show, not business. Cattle dealers were happy to sell the Osage high-priced livestock, and local businesspeople welcomed the spending sprees that occurred when the tribal families entertained.

An Osage woman prepares food next to her automobile. Oil wealth resulted in a mix of luxury and tradition.

In 1926 and 1927 the Osage invited the Society of American Indians, an intertribal social organization, to hold its second and third annual conventions in Pawhuska. In those years the tribe requested payment of its quarterly royalties 10 days early to spend on lavish preparations. Seventy cattle were slaughtered and barbecued for the guests. The Osage staged parades, archery contests, rodeos, hand games, dances, a golf tournament, and a beauty contest (in 1927 a mixed-blood Osage was crowned queen) to supplement the convention's business meetings.

The Osage also used their wealth in the national interest. Many joined other Indians in enthusiastically supporting the war effort during World War I. Approximately 120 full-bloods and scores of mixed-bloods served in the armed forces. Many joined Oklahoma's National Guard, whose Company E became known as the Millionaire Company because of its ranks of wealthy Osage, Choctaw, and Creek. In 1924 President Calvin Coolidge presented a certificate to the Osage, lauding their "unswerving Loyalty and Patriotism" on the battlefield and on the home front, where their financial contributions to the Red Cross and purchase of war bonds exceeded those of their non-Indian neighbors.

The Osage historian John Joseph Mathews found little to praise about the 1920s boom years. He deplored the fact that many Osage turned to liquor as an escape from the confusion and pressures caused by oil wealth. During Prohibition, when a constitutional amendment prohibited the manufacture and sale of alcoholic beverages, al-

President Calvin Coolidge presents Chief Fred Lookout with a certificate recognizing the tribe's contributions in World War I. The Osage strongly supported the war effort both at home and abroad.

coholism was the biggest health problem among the Osage. In Pawhuska the agency superintendent reported that "the bootleggers have become very bold," and that it was "a daily occurrence" to find intoxicated Osage.

Under Indian Commissioner Cato Sells, an ardent prohibitionist, the fight against excessive drinking among all Indians was stepped up. In 1915 he had eliminated the carnival-like atmosphere of the Osage's quarterly payment days, which even before 1900 had attracted confidence men, thieves, bootleggers, and eager salesmen of mostly worthless items. Often entire payments were spent or lost through trickery or rob-

bery in only one or two days. Sells insisted that checks be mailed directly to most tribal members; those who could not receive theirs by mail could collect them at Indian camps in Pawhuska, Hominy, and Gray Horse, where outsiders were not allowed.

For many non-Indian inhabitants of Osage County, the Osage were among the area's natural resources, like grazing land and petroleum. One newspaper, the *Hominy News-Republican*, boasted about being a community of "1,000 white people and 900 Osage Indians drawing thousands of dollars yearly." Few non-Indians were troubled by the blatant exploitation of the Osage. Most justified the process of separating the Indians from their money by saying that the Osage had done nothing to earn their wealth and that their failure to protect it represented laziness or the stubborn refusal to learn non-Indian ways.

The Osage's primary protection against exploitation rested with the federal government, which was obligated to look after the tribe's interests. Unfortunately, the protection was limited. Although the agency-sponsored auctions resulted in fair prices for Osage oil, most of the allotted surface land quickly slipped out of Indian hands. The 1906 allotment act empowered the secretary of the interior to issue certificates of competency to adult members of the tribe. Those found to be of sound mind and who demonstrated an ability to read, write, and speak English well enough to conduct business could be declared legally responsible for their own property. They were then able to sell or lease all their lands, including that of their underage children, and make investments or purchases of any kind.

Between 1907 and 1929, thousands of acres of formerly restricted land were sold or leased to non-Indian farmers and ranchers. Thousands more were leased without formal contracts by Osage, certified as "competent," who did not understand the actual value of their land or the obligations of contracts. In addition, the Indians lost much of their land through numerous swindles contrived by non-Indians seeking to gain control of the property.

Swindles also drained the Indians of vast sums of money. Investigations revealed that millions of dollars were misappropriated by "guardians," the local lawyers and business owners appointed to handle the business affairs of Osage who were declared incompetent. Some storekeepers sold their Indian wards goods they did not need at three and four times their actual price. Bankers who were guardians made loans at outrageous interest rates. Other guardians took kickbacks for bringing in business to car dealers, who sold cars to the Osage at premium prices. Even doctors had a higher fee schedule for Osage than non-Indians. Of 25 lawsuits filed in 1924 by the Interior Department against dishonest guardians for recovery of Osage money, none went to trial—all the defendants made out-of-court settlements to avoid criminal prosecution.

Another popular way for non-Indians to get rich was to marry an Osage allottee. The agency received many inquiries about the possibility of marriage to an Osage. In one, a Missouri farmer, who offered to pay the superintendent $25 for every $5,000 that an Osage bride could bring him in marriage, observed that "marriage is as much a business matter as anything else."

Perhaps the most sinister attempt to cash in on the Osage's wealth was contrived by several non-Indians living in Fairfax, a community near the Indian village of Gray Horse. The "Osage Reign of Terror," as the plot was called by the newspapers, brought the Fed-

```
30 | OCT 18 1907
     OSAGE INDIAN AGENCY, OKLA.        Joplin, Mo.  10/16/07.
INDIAN AGENT
        Pawhuska, Okla.
DEAR SIR:--
             I am a young man with good habits and none
of the bad, with several thousand dollars, and want a
good indian girl for a wife.  I am sober, honest,
industrious man and stand well in my community.

             I want a woman between the ages of 18
and 35 years of age, not a full blood, but prefer one
as near white as possible.

             I lived on a farm most of my life and know
how to gets results from a farm as well as a mercantile
business.  Having means it is natural I want some one
my equal financially as well as socially.  If you can
place me in correspondence with a good woman and I succeed
in marrying her for every Five Thousand Dollars she is
worth I will give you Twenty Five Dollars.  If she is
worth 25,000  you would get $125 if I got her.
             This is a plain business proposition and
I trust you will consider it as such.  You have every
facility to know them and help me.  Now will you?
General Delivery.            C. T. Plimer

P. S.--
         I will furnish them with every facility to in-
vestigate me as to what I am worth, my standing, etc.
I am not a pauper or worthless being, but what I claim
but believe marriage is as much of a business matter as
anything else, or else it is likely to be a failure.
                             C.T. Plimer
```

A letter from a Missouri farmer to the Osage agent offering payment for an arranged marriage to an Indian woman.

eral Bureau of Investigation to Osage County and directly influenced the passage of special legislation to protect the Osage people.

The plot apparently originated with William K. Hale, Fairfax's most prominent citizen. Hale had arrived on the reservation around 1900, a cowboy like dozens of others employed by cattle raisers to drive herds from Texas to Kansas, pausing in Indian Territory to fatten trail-worn cattle. On a return trip, he had remained on the reservation instead of going back to Texas. He hired himself out to an Osage family and lived with them illegally in the Gray Horse Indian settlement.

Hale prospered and became a well-known and popular figure whose wealth, political influence, and easygoing personality toward non-Indian and Indian alike earned him the title "King of the Osage Hills." Once established, he invited relatives to move from Texas to Fairfax. His nephew, Ernest Burkhart, was among those who came. Burkhart, a veteran of World War I, married a full-blood Osage, Mollie Kyle, whose mother, Lizzie Q, held three headrights. Mollie and her two sisters, Anna Brown and Rita Smith, were original allottees collecting their own shares of oil and gas royalties. They and members of their extended family had reputations as gamblers and drinkers. Hale contrived to have Mollie's family killed by poisoning liquor that the authorities would assume to be tainted bootleg alcohol. Burkhart, through his wife's inheritance, would then gain control of several headright incomes.

Hale and Burkhart hired local outlaws to eliminate their victims. After several were killed as planned, the strategy was ruined when, on May 28, 1921, the body of Anna Brown was found at the bottom of a canyon near Fairfax, a bullet lodged in her head. Two months later Lizzie Q died from poisoned liquor, and soon afterward a relative, Henry Roan, was found shot to death in his car. Finally and most spectacularly, Rita Smith, her husband,

and a servant were killed when a nitro-glycerin charge demolished their Fair-fax home.

FBI agents began an undercover investigation of the murders, but could find no hard evidence implicating Hale. He misled the authorities by serving as a pallbearer at Anna Brown's funeral and offering a reward for her killers, and he had covered his connection with the murders by hiring a second group of killers to eliminate the original ones. The weak link in Hale's conspiracy was Burkhart, who was convinced by the FBI to admit his part in the scheme and testified against his uncle. Despite Burkhart's damaging evidence, Hale's money and influence prevented quick justice. Three trials were held over four years before he was convicted in 1929. The reign of terror ended, but more than a dozen murders connected to the case were left unsolved.

After Hale's first trial, the federal government, moved by the violence, passed legislation in February 1925 that made it impossible for a person convicted of causing the death of an Osage Indian to inherit an allotment share. The law further provided that only heirs of Indian blood could inherit from Osage with one-half or more blood quantums and stipulated that the beneficiaries of headright holders with less than one-half Osage blood would upon inheritance be required to sell their shares to the tribe. The cost of the shares would be based on their estimated worth. After that, no non-Indian could hope to inherit a headright.

Osage chief Bacon Rind and his wives.

During the murder trials in 1926, a Tulsa newspaper chided the residents of Osage County for not having exerted themselves to apprehend the murderers earlier. County newspapers retorted that only a few persons were involved, ignoring the fact that the entire population lived directly or indirectly on money generated by Osage headright payments. Chief Bacon Rind, disgusted with his non-Indian neighbors, probably spoke for most Osage when he said, "There are men amongst the whites, honest men, but they are mighty scarce—mighty few."▲

While visiting the tribe, Catlin painted this scene of an Osage roping a wild pony.

THE
DEPRESSION
YEARS

In the fall of 1929, prices on the stock market, which had skyrocketed during the prosperous 1920s, declined sharply. The incomes of the corporations, banks, and individuals who had invested heavily in the market declined as well. Industry stagnated, and the nation slipped into an economic depression. In the decade that followed, thousands of banks and businesses failed, and millions of people were unemployed and penniless.

In 1930 two leaders, sensing that new changes were about to confront the tribe, advised the Osage on how to survive the effects of the Great Depression. The first leader was an elderly full-blood, Henry Pratt (Nopawalla); the second was George Wright, the non-Indian Osage superintendent. Pratt, who spoke over a Pawhuska radio station, recalled moving from Kansas to Oklahoma and running away from boarding school. "In those days," he said, "we had strong red blood . . . but now our blood is getting white, through

intermarrying with the white man." He urged the Osage youth to get an education so they could understand their future, "the hard, white highway of the white man." Superintendent Wright, who was leaving the agency after 16 years, also advised the Osage that, "as the whites are here to stay, you must learn to deal with them." Speaking from experience, he reasoned that "the white man will not deliberately take advantage of you, but it is human nature to take advantage of the other fellow if he can." He urged the Indians to rely on his successor and the mixed-bloods for help.

Changes came quickly. The Osage's journey along the "hard, white highway" now continued with less cash to pave the way. The prices of most commodities, including oil and natural gas, dropped sharply, greatly reducing the amount of Osage headright payments. Meanwhile, government restrictions on the production of oil, aimed at stabilizing the price of petroleum, limited the

Henry Pratt (Nopawalla), whose wisdom helped guide the Osage through the Great Depression. He wears the traditional beaver bandeau of the Osage and carries a Peyote ceremony fan.

yield of Osage wells, which reduced the tribe's royalties further. From a high of $13,200 in 1925, headright payments decreased yearly through 1932, when they reached a low of $585. Payments then rose somewhat, but the annual average for the 1930s was only $1,500. In 1939 more than a million acres of oil-rich land were still unleased and production continued to be sluggish because of an inactive market.

The non-Indian community in Osage County also felt the loss of tribal income. With less money to spend, Indian patronage declined, and many businesses owned by non-Indians faltered. To save their livelihood, the non-Indians unsuccessfully tried to persuade hundreds of mixed-bloods who had fled the alcoholism, violence, and unsafe atmosphere on the reservation during the 1920s to return home. As early as 1923, the agency had been mailing headright checks to more than 100 addresses outside Oklahoma. Most Osage had relocated to Kansas, Missouri, Arkansas, California (especially the southern part of that state), and other areas of Oklahoma. Some, however, left the country for locations as varied as Mexico, France, China, and Japan.

Despite their reduced finances, those Osage living on the reservation continued to be exploited throughout the 1930s. Corrupt guardians allowed incompetent Osage to spend until they were flat broke. Outright robbery and theft actually increased as the Indian camps at Pawhuska, Hominy, and Gray Horse became the special targets of criminals. To aid the single federal law officer assigned to the county, the agency hired three law officers, whose salaries were paid with tribal funds, to be stationed at the camps.

Alcoholism continued to be a problem among the Osage during the 1930s, and many also became dependent upon drugs, especially morphine and marijuana. The seizure of a cache of drugs worth $50,000 in Osage County in 1930 was the largest confiscation in state history until after World War II. As early as 1932, federal agents estimated that 75 Osage who had been judged incompetent and had restrictions placed on their spending were drug addicts and that many whose spending was unrestricted were habitual users as well. According to agency statistics, between 1930 and 1934, 42 Osage died as a result of car accidents, fights, overdoses, illnesses, and other alcohol- and drug-related incidents. It must be remembered that for most of these four years liquor was still considered an illegal substance (Prohibition was repealed in 1933).

In 1934 the council appealed to Congress for a special liquor and drug law for Osage County that would make these substances illegal, but it was turned down. Speaking before the council, one disenchanted full-blood, John Abbott, said, "Think they allotted us too quick. We ought to build a wall around Osage County, have gates, make white man pay $1 apiece; we took up ways of the white man too quick."

By 1935 much of the Osage's land had passed from their hands. Less than a third of the 1,470,000 acres allotted in 1907 was still owned by members of the tribe, and most of that land belonged to Osage possessing at least one headright. A severe drought in the 1930s had transformed much of Oklahoma, including Osage County's once-fertile farm and grazing land, into a dust bowl. The resulting decline in income from

Farm machinery in Cimarron County, Oklahoma, lies idle, buried by the sandstorms that turned most of the prairie into a vast wasteland during the 1930s.

A farmer in the Oklahoma dust bowl lifts part of a fence to keep it from being submerged under drifting sand.

leased surface land and decrease in the food supply strained the Osage even further. Families trying to support large numbers of unallotted children on reduced headright incomes had an especially hard time getting by, but young adults with only fractions of headrights or none at all suffered the most.

A census taken in 1939 revealed the extent of the tribe's loss of affluence: Of the 3,672 enrolled Osage, more than a third, 1,418, received no money at all from tribal sources. Another 1,047 drew only fractions of headright incomes from inherited allotment shares. The re-

maining 1,207 were original allottees receiving full headright shares, of whom 875 were competent and 332 legally incompetent, with restrictions placed on their spending.

Perhaps the most emotionally devastated by the depression were the tribal mixed-bloods who had left the reservation. Aided by their physical similarity to whites, their education, and their headright income, many had assimilated into the non-Indian culture. Faced with drastic reductions in their headright payments and widespread failure of the investments and businesses they had established in their new homes, some previously well-to-do mixed-bloods returned to Osage County in the early 1930s. The Osage sense of communal welfare obligated the tribespeople to take in any member in need, and the mixed-bloods who returned knew they would be cared for by the tribe. Once there, they were dismayed to discover their families and friends also struggling to maintain themselves.

Mixed-bloods and full-bloods alike turned to their tribal council for relief. The Osage council now had to deal with matters less pleasurable than the approval of lucrative oil and gas leases. During these difficult years two leaders emerged to guide the Osage through their hardships. Chief Fred Lookout, a full-blood, represented the old in Osage life; council member John Joseph Mathews, a mixed-blood, represented the new.

Little is known of Fred Lookout's childhood. He spoke of accompanying his father on buffalo hunts when he was a youngster and of receiving the name Wy-hah-shah-shin-kah, Little-Eagle-That-Gets-What-He-Wants, but he always refused to tell the story behind the name's origins. His father had been a leading figure of his clan and band, probably one reason why the agent Laban Miles chose Fred along with a dozen other Osage children to attend Carlisle boarding school in Pennsylvania.

Lookout returned from school in 1884 just weeks before his father died. On the advice of an uncle he remained

Chief Fred Lookout was one of the Osage's most revered leaders. He served 32 consecutive years as principal chief, more than any elected official in Osage history.

on the reservation. He married an Osage woman, Julia Pryor, and they lived on a small farm near Pawhuska. When the eldest of their four children became ill and died, the Lookouts grieved in the traditional Osage way, giving all their possessions to others and leaving their home for months to roam the reserve, where they were sheltered and fed by members of the tribe. When they finally returned to their house, Lookout began a more public life that would lead to his being

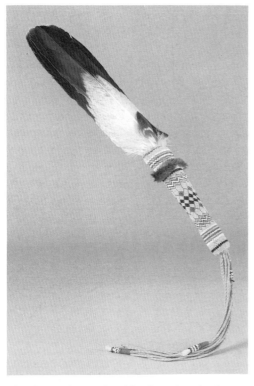

An Osage fan made of leather, fur, feathers, and beads that was used in Peyote ceremonies.

recognized as both a spiritual and political leader.

Like many other Osage in the 1890s, Lookout had become a member of the Native American Church, a combination of traditional Indian beliefs and Christianity. Forced relocation and constant subjection to the government's civilization program had left many Indians yearning for spiritual comfort against, and possibly deliverance from, their oppressors. To some Indians, the Peyote religion of the Native American Church offered the reaffirmation they

sought. Followers of this belief ingested the buttons of the peyote cactus (a plant native to the extreme southwestern region of the United States) as a sacrament similar to the Christian elements of wine and bread. Lookout became a roadman, a leader of Peyote ceremonies, and would remain active for the rest of his life. (Osage membership in the church gradually declined after World War I; by 1980 there would be only 150 active Osage Peyotists.)

As was often the case in tribal politics, Lookout got his political start through a family connection. His wife was a second cousin of Chief James Bigheart, and "Big Jim" made Fred his political protégé. In 1908, around the time that Bigheart died, Lookout was elected to a two-year term as assistant principal chief. He did not run for office in 1910 or 1912 but ran successfully for principal chief in 1914. He was reelected in 1916. At the end of that term he quit the council until 1924, when he was again elected principal chief. He served two more two-year terms, then was elected to consecutive four-year terms beginning in 1930 and continuing until his death in 1956. Lookout's 32 consecutive years in office would be the longest of any elected person in Osage history.

Lookout, an astute politician, had to shift his position on a key issue in order to be reelected in 1934. In that election four political parties fielded candidates for the Osage council. There were 645 voters. (According to the 1906 allotment act, only males over 21 years old who were original allottees could cast ballots.) Of these, 165 were full-bloods, which meant that the mixed-bloods could control the outcome even if their votes were split among the four parties' candidates. Lookout realized that the Osage needed a full-blood leader—or at least a person who appeared to be a full-blood—to win the support of both the older full-bloods and the younger mixed-bloods and maintain the solidarity of the tribe. To ensure that this would happen, Lookout and other full-bloods considered ways of redefining the meaning of full-blood or reaching an understanding with the mixed-bloods that would assure full-blood principal and assistant chiefs regardless of the council majority.

The full-bloods decided to broaden their political base by identifying as full-blood all Osage of one-half or more blood quantums. Some Osage with lesser blood heritages were also accepted into the classification if their physical appearance and/or cultural behavior resembled that of full-bloods. Chief Lookout easily won reelection in 1934 and another full-blood, Harry Kohpay, became his assistant chief. Two full-bloods and six mixed-bloods were elected to the council.

One of the newly elected mixed-blood council members was 40-year-old John Joseph Mathews. The eldest of five children, Mathews had a one-eighth degree of Osage blood: His grandmother had been half Osage. His father, William Mathews, had prospered in Pawhuska as a trader and later

a banker. Young Mathews grew up in a stone house on Agency Hill overlooking the town. He learned to speak somewhat haltingly in Osage and mingled with the tribespeople who shopped in his father's store. Mathews spent much of his youth riding, hunting, and camping, often visiting the lodges of Osage who continued to live in the traditional manner. Later he would always carefully distinguish between the mixed-bloods and full-bloods within the tribe, ascribing different cultural and psychological traits to each group.

As a council member Mathews quickly proved that he grasped the realities of his tribe. During a discussion about the exploitation of the Osage, he gave a clear-cut analysis of how they had become the chief support of the non-Indian population. "If the payments were stopped tomorrow," Mathews said, "there would be nothing here [in Pawhuska] in six months, there would be coyotes howling in the streets."

Chief Lookout, Mathews, and the other members of the council elected in 1934 faced the need to help their fellow tribespeople through the depression. Indians all over the country were in desperate straits: Between 1928 and 1932, the per capita income of Indians dropped from approximately $200 a year to $81. In April 1933 John Collier, a longtime activist for the rights of Indians, had been appointed commissioner of Indian affairs to design and administer an Indian New Deal to de-

Mixed-blood council member John Joseph Mathews (center), flanked by Principal Chief Fred Lookout and Lookout's wife, Julia. Mathews, who had attended Oxford University in England, wrote about the Osage in books that earned him national recognition.

velop work skills and create jobs that would bring relief and recovery to the nation's suffering tribes.

Collier devised a plan that marked a sharp change from past Indian policy. Previously, the government had concentrated its efforts on Americanizing the Indians; now Collier wanted to help revitalize tribal governments and traditional cultures. He hoped that the Indian New Deal, offering programs similar to those available to non-Indi-

ans, would relieve immediate economic distress and that individuals and families could learn to aid themselves and achieve economic recovery.

While the plan, formulated in Congress as the Wheeler-Howard Bill and signed into law as the Indian Reorganization Act (IRA), was being debated in Congress, Commissioner Collier traveled nationwide to gain Indian support for the proposed legislation. The bill stipulated that before any tribe would

OSAGE RENAISSANCE MAN

The Osage historian John Joseph Mathews exemplified the merging of Indian and non-Indian cultures. After attending public schools in Pawhuska, Mathews went to the University of Oklahoma, where he majored in geology. His studies were interrupted for nearly three years by World War I, in which he served as an aviator. When he graduated in 1920, he was offered a prestigious Rhodes scholarship to Oxford University in England. He rejected the scholarship because, as an original allottee, he did not need the financial aid; however, he did attend Oxford, earning a degree in natural science.

Mathews returned to Osage County to live in 1929, but he continued to travel regularly, most often on hunting trips that he wrote about in brief articles and short stories. In 1932 the University of Oklahoma Press published his informal historical sketch of the Osage, *Wah'Kon-Tah; The Osage and the White Man's Road*. The book was chosen by the Book-of-the-Month Club and sold well. Inspired by its success, Mathews wrote four more books: *Osages: Children of the Middle Waters, Talking to the Moon, Sundown,* and *Life and Death of an Oilman: The Career of E. W. Marland*.

Even though he received a headright income, Mathews disliked many of the effects of oil wealth on the Osage. In his largely autobiographical novel *Sundown*, he wrote, "Slowly from the east the black oil derricks crept toward the west, rising from the blackjacks, like some unnatural growth from the diseased tissues of the earth."

Despite the popularity of his books and his involvement in tribal politics, Mathews lived a reclusive life. He built a small stone house on a forested ridge eight miles outside of Pawhuska, where he continued to live until failing health forced him to move into town in the 1970s. He died in Pawhuska in 1978.

John Joseph Mathews at his home near Pawhuska.

come under the program, a majority of its members would have to vote in favor of it. Collier's visit to the Oklahoma tribes turned into a series of debates. Indians who had kept their allotments and worked on them, and acculturated Indians with education and jobs, viewed Collier's plan as unprogressive and backward looking. Many Oklahoma Indians resisted the new legislation because, after decades of disappointment, they were suspicious of any federal policy. Mathews, a strong supporter of the IRA, wrote and spoke on behalf of the legislation, and Chief Lookout, who also favored it, pre-

sided over an informational meeting held in Pawhuska in 1934.

Despite these efforts the Oklahoma tribes were not included in the IRA, which was signed into law in 1934. However, two years later, Oklahoma Indians were included in essentially the same federal programs under the Oklahoma Indian Welfare Act. Only the Osage tribe was excluded from the new act, even though they had voted in favor of it. As had happened with the IRA, members of Osage County's non-Indian community who realized that the shared tribal economy proposed in the legislation was not in their best

Members of the Osage council that governed the tribe during the 1930s.

interests lobbied against the act and exerted control over politicians in Washington. Outside of Alaska, the Osage was the only tribe recognized by the U.S. government to be formally left out of the Indian New Deal.

Nevertheless, the tribe did participate in some relief and recovery programs. The council applied for government funding and, with additional money from oil and gas royalties, initiated an ambitious agricultural extension system, a health clinic, and a social-work office. On behalf of the tribe, Mathews wrote a grant proposal for $25,000 to construct a building to house a tribal museum and meeting hall for the council and other Osage organizations. The Works Progress Administration, a government agency, approved the grant, and the building, dedicated in 1938, was the first tribally owned and administered museum in the nation.

Throughout the 1930s Chief Lookout willingly allowed Mathews and the other young mixed-bloods on the council to take the initiative in dealing with the world outside the Osage community. He consistently calmed the older full-bloods who resented their increasingly secondary role in setting tribal policy and constantly smoothed over differences between the full-bloods and

Josephine Pryor Hamilton, Osage artist in ribbon appliqué and proprietor of a crafts shop in Pawhuska. The Indian New Deal stressed the revitalization of traditional cultures and encouraged work in arts and crafts.

mixed-bloods. Lookout, speaking as usual through an interpreter, although his English was fairly fluent, challenged mixed-bloods like Mathews to be cultural brokers for their tribe. He said, "If you let your white man tongues say what is in your Indian hearts you will do great things for your people." ▲

Tal-lee, one of the most distinguished and respected warriors of the tribe, with his lance in his hand, his shield on his arm, and his bow and quiver slung over his back.

WAR, WEALTH,
AND
CHANGES

On December 7, 1941, the Japanese attacked the U.S. naval base at Pearl Harbor, Hawaii, triggering the United States's involvement in World War II. The U.S. government declared war the next day, but in Osage County the war drums had sounded mere hours after the bombing was reported over the radio, summoning the Osage to repel the enemy.

Memories of Osage triumphs in World War I had been kept alive through commemorative dances and other observances that reinforced a half-remembered warrior tradition. For most Osage, going to war reflected their almost mystical bond with the land: They would fight to defend a birthright sanctioned by countless generations, rather than to uphold a learned belief in the abstract principle of democracy.

Chief Fred Lookout presided over a series of ceremonies in which traditional warriors' names were bestowed on the tribe's men, and—in a significant departure from tradition—women who

entered the armed forces. According to Superintendent Theodore Hall, 381 Osage were in military uniform in April 1943. Most prominent among them was Clarence L. Tinker, a mixed-blood who rose to the rank of major general in the army air corps. He was the first Indian to reach that rank since Stand Watie, a Cherokee who had served in the Confederate army during the Civil War. Tinker was killed in an airplane crash in 1942. He was posthumously awarded the Distinguished Service Medal, and an air force base near Oklahoma City was renamed Tinker Field to honor his memory.

On the home front Osage support for the war effort was strong. More than 200 Osage were employed in airplane factories in Tulsa. Residents of Osage County bought war bonds in large quantities, collected scrap metal, rolled bandages, and staged victory dances to celebrate the tribe's participation in the fighting. With money from tribal funds, the Osage paid for a training plane for

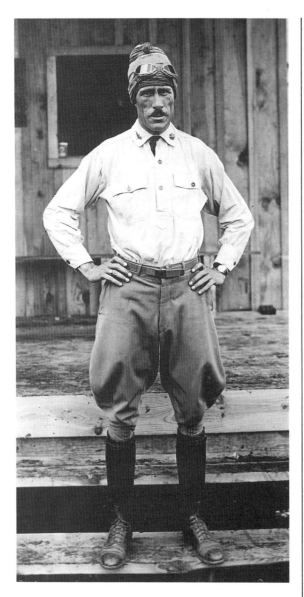

Major General Clarence L. Tinker was the senior Army officer in charge of reorganizing U.S. air forces after the Japanese attack of December 7, 1941, on Pearl Harbor, Hawaii. He was killed at the Battle of Midway in the Pacific in June 1942.

the air corps, negotiating the terms with their characteristic flair for business.

World War II ushered in a new era of political, social, and economic changes for the Osage. As long as the original allottees had been a majority, the tribe felt a shared cultural heritage, and tribal politics remained fairly stable. However, as members of the allotted generation died, they began to be outnumbered by the growing group of unallotted Osage born after 1907. Now possession of a headright or the likelihood of inheriting one separated a minority of Osage from those who had an insignificant headright fraction or none at all. This division between haves, who owned headrights, and have-nots, who did not, added to and complicated old dislikes arising out of family and clan disputes and mutual distrust between the mixed-bloods and full-bloods. In addition, geographical and cultural splits arose between those Osage living in Osage County and those living elsewhere.

Provision for the future of unallotted Osage youth continued to be an issue within the tribe, as it had even before World War II. In 1917, realizing that future generations of Osage had been excluded from sharing the tribe's mineral wealth, Chief Lookout and other council members had strongly supported a resolution calling for the participation of allottees' children born after July 1, 1907, in all future oil and gas royalties. Lookout was apprehensive that opening the roll to include these young Osage would create dissension within the tribe, and he was right. Paul Red Eagle, the assistant chief, and Harry Bayliss, a mixed-blood councilman, favored the resolution. Wah-sho-shah, a full-blood council member, denounced it as a "half-breed scheme" to admit fraudulent applicants, as had occurred in 1906. After a lengthy council debate no clear consensus was reached, and the resolution died.

The status of women in Osage society also changed as war, wealth, and the right to vote gave them more social, economic, and political power. Osage women's shares in the tribe's mineral holdings and surface land had given them an economic independence exceptional among both Indian and non-Indian women at that time. Divorced and widowed women were especially affected by the changes in status brought on by wealth. In the past, women in these categories had been virtually excluded from the mainstream of Osage life, acceptable only as mates for non-Indians. By 1920 many divorced and widowed women maintained households of their own, often serving as the sole financial supporter of children as well as of younger relatives eager for their favor and possibly their inheritances.

It took the tribeswomen somewhat longer to achieve political recognition. Before allotment only one woman, Rosana Chouteau, had played a significant role in tribal government. During the 1870s she had been second chief of the Beaver band. The men of the band

Esther Quinton Cheshewalla, a mixed-blood Osage, was one of the first Indian women in the nation to join the U.S. Marine Corps during World War II. She is shown here in one of the airplanes she helped repair. Their participation in the war effort increased the status of women in the tribe.

NOTABLE
OSAGE WOMEN

Three Osage women have been performing artists in the 20th century, and one of them achieved international fame. The first was Angela Gorman, who studied in New York and became a noted opera singer in the 1920s. Her performing career was advanced enough that in 1919 the tribe honored her achievements. In a ceremony conducted by Chief Fred Lookout, Gorman was given the name Eagle Maiden, reflecting her membership in the eagle clan. "I must prove the qualities of my ancestry as well as be the pioneer blazing the trail for other girls in the tribe," she said.

Among those other Osage girls were the half-blood sisters Maria and Marjorie Tallchief, who both became noted ballet dancers. Maria, born in 1925 in Fairfax, Oklahoma, would be hailed by dance critics as "the finest American-born classic ballerina the 20th century has produced." She was also one of the first. When Maria was seven years old, the Tallchief family moved to Los Angeles, where she studied piano and dance. She was so torn between these two performing arts that in her debut she played piano for half of the program and danced the other half. After graduating from high school in 1942, she was accepted into the Ballet Russe de Monte Carlo, at that time the leading classical dance company in the United States, and quickly gained recognition. She married dancer/choreographer George Balanchine in 1946 and the following year joined his new company, which became the New York City Ballet in 1948. Meanwhile her sister, Marjorie Tallchief, was among several Americans who were principal dancers with the new Grand Ballet de Monte Carlo in Europe.

During the 1950s, Maria Tallchief was the leading female interpreter of Balanchine's work, creating roles in some of his most notable ballets of the period. Following her divorce from Balanchine, she felt she was not being given the leading roles she deserved. In 1960 she left the company to join the American Ballet Theatre as principal dancer and later was a leading ballerina with the Hamburg State Opera in Germany and director of the Lyric Opera Ballet in Chicago, where, after retiring as a performer, she also taught dance. Throughout her career, Maria Tallchief did much to bring ballet to the attention of the American public, performing on television and in national tours. In 1960 she received the *Dance* magazine award for her achievements.

Principal Chief Fred Lookout (standing, center) supported a proposal in 1917 to open the tribal roll to the children of Osage allottees. Wah-sho-shah (standing, left) opposed the idea. With them are Petsemore (seated) and Henry Red Eagle.

had chosen her in part because she was a relative of another chief, but more importantly because of the leadership she showed in encouraging her band to accept the U.S. government's civilization program as a means to survival in the non-Indian world. In 1922 two mixed-blood sisters, Corine and Leona Girard, both original allottees, appealed to the Bureau of Indian Affairs for help in obtaining voting rights for Osage women. The bureau urged the Osage council to allow allotted women to vote and hold office, but the council rejected the idea.

Little more was heard about the issue until 1938, when a group of tribeswomen circulated a petition among the Osage requesting that women be allowed to vote. Again the council decided against the proposal. Not until 1941 did the council finally accept women's suffrage. Ten more years would pass before a woman was nominated for the council. Although the number of female candidates increased in the 1950s and 1960s, it was not until 1976 that the first woman, a mixed-blood named Camille Pangburn, was elected.

The expansion of the Osage electorate to include women helped ease some internal dissension, but economic and social factors continued to plague the tribe and affect its politics. Attempts to alter the council's organization were seen by holders of headrights, the only people eligible to vote, as ploys to upset the delicately balanced political arrangement. According to the 1906 allotment act, the council was to exist until January 1, 1959. In 1957 a bill was introduced into the U.S. House of Representatives to extend its life to January 1, 1984. Several dissatisfied groups within the tribe attempted to use this legislation to promote reforms, especially to grant the right to vote to all adult Osage without headrights. But this and other suggestions failed, and the bill as enacted merely extended the life of the council. Long before the January 1, 1984, deadline, Congress voted to extend the life of the council indefinitely.

In the 1960s and early 1970s dissatisfaction with the tribal government increased within the tribe. More and more Osage were excluded from participation in their own tribal council because only persons owning full or partial headrights were allowed to vote and hold office. Many young unallotted Osage and nonheadright holders were resentful because they felt that they had a greater biological and cultural claim to inclusion in the tribe than some headright holders did. A warring group of full-blood allottees, uncomfortable with the knowledge that to outsiders the Osage identity was overshadowed by the fame of oil wealth, was also unhappy at the council's preoccupation with preserving the tribe's claim to the mineral reserves.

In 1964 representatives of these groups formed a grievance committee, calling themselves the Osage Nation Organization (ONO). Membership was limited to persons over 21 years old who possessed at least one-fourth Osage blood quantum. From an initial 250 members in 1965, membership in ONO increased to about 800 in the early 1970s. According to one leader, Raymond Lasley, the ONO took its name from the members' conviction that the legitimate Osage tribe had gone out of existence when the secretary of the interior abolished the tribal constitution in 1900. The ONO cited the tribe's exclusion from New Deal legislation in the 1930s as further justification for its position. Leroy Logan, a full-blood and an ONO founder, referred to the "no bloods" (those non-Osage who were fraudulently enrolled in 1907) who, he said, "stole our name and our tribe. We can't be the Osage tribe, so we called ourselves the Osage Nation Organization."

The ONO sought to change the structure of tribal government by gaining voting rights for all Osage over 21 years old and limiting membership on the council to tribespeople with at least one-quarter Osage blood. The group hoped to create a new council that would function like those of other tribes, most of which required council members to possess at least one-quarter—and often one-half—Indian blood, and not merely serve as a business committee. In 1971 a federal commission investigated the existing Osage government and recommended some changes to provide equal representation for all members of the tribe. But in the first 25 years of the ONO's existence no substantial changes were made, although modifications in the old system may well occur in the future, especially as the organization continues to exert pressure for them.

In 1964 Congress passed legislation extending the tribe's rights to its mineral reserves indefinitely, thus assuring it permanent control of its major resource. Although oil and gas profits were never again as great as they had been in the 1920s, headright income remained high through the mid-1960s. New mineral discoveries outside the United States depressed the oil market in the late 1960s and early 1970s, driving down prices until the income from a headright was reduced to a few hundred dollars annually. When an embargo by oil-producing countries in the Middle East suddenly closed off the flow of foreign oil in 1973, the Osage fields were rejuvenated. Headright income rose from about $3,000 per person in 1973 to nearly $12,000 in 1977 and more than $26,000 by 1980. The collapse of the embargo a few years later decreased the output of the Osage fields and eventually caused some wells to cease production altogether. By 1983 headright income was half of what it had been in 1980, and it continued to drop in succeeding years.

Oil wealth also affected other areas of Osage life. Headright payments contributed to the perpetuation of the traditional extended family, sometimes with adverse effects. Parents, children, grandparents, and assorted nieces, nephews, uncles, and aunts often

The official seal of the Osage tribe. The Osage Nation Organization holds that the true tribe ceased to exist in 1900.

shared one or more headright incomes, and many avoided seeking employment even after royalty payments were reduced in the 1930s. According to an anthropologist who lived in Osage County in the 1960s, some tribal mothers actually discouraged their children from taking jobs in order to keep them dependent on the family allotment checks and thus subject to maternal domination.

Some customs and traditions underwent alterations as a result of oil wealth. The traditional war-mourning ceremony disappeared before World War I, but tribespeople today continue to honor their dead with elaborate rituals. Most full-bloods and many mixed-bloods still hold a funeral feast to honor

An Osage bride of the 1890s, on her way to the groom's house to be married. Traditionally, women were transported to their wedding astride a horse.

a dead relative as well as a memorial feast a year after the death. In the 1930s the agency tried to limit the costs of these feasts to $1,000 per event, about one-third of what was normally spent, but lavish spending continued in families who could afford it.

Marriage negotiations and weddings also changed. Even the earliest agents in Indian Territory had strongly discouraged arranged marriages of very young Osage girls, but the full-bloods persisted in the practice until 1910. By the 1920s, time, money, and the growing independence of the tribe's young people led to the decline of the lengthy sequence of negotiations between the families of the bride and groom and the consolidation of the four days of celebration following the marriage into two. Osage marriages of the 1920s illustrate how the tribespeople used their wealth to preserve traditions while at the same time adapting to non-Indian ways. At the marriage of one prominent full-blood in 1927, the bride and 10 bridesmaids were transported to the groom's residence in 4 luxury automobiles, but the horses that traditionally carried the bridal party also accompanied the caravan. Upon their arrival, the bride and her attendants were carried into the house on blankets supported by the groom's family, and an elaborate feast was held. Traditionally a marriage became official at the end of the feast, but at this wedding a Catholic priest performed a brief marriage service.

This mix of traditional and non-Indian features in marriage ceremonies occurred less frequently in the 1930s and died out during World War II. In the 1970s mixed rites were revived by some young Osage seeking to reestablish certain aspects of Osage culture, especially the wearing of traditional

A typical Osage wedding in the 1930s. The members of the bridal party wear tunics and top hats adorned with silver bands and ostrich feathers. These outfits, which had been popular with the Osage for more than 50 years, were derived from U.S. military uniforms of the early 19th century.

Dancers, dressed in traditional costumes, participate in the I'N-Lon-Schka dances, held every spring. The drummers, seated in the background, do not wear ceremonial clothes.

Osage wedding garb. During Thomas Jefferson's presidency a delegation of Osage chiefs had visited Washington, D.C., and had been given military uniforms and top hats as presents. The chiefs gave the clothing to their wives and daughters, and somehow the custom of wearing these uniforms as part of the bridal attire had been started. By the 1880s brides and their attendants were wearing military tunics trimmed with gold epaulettes, top hats adorned with silver bands and dyed feathers, floor-length woolen skirts, and moccasins.

The most widely observed Osage tradition today is the I'N-Lon-Schka dances. Held each spring, the dances celebrate the selection of a young boy as tribal drumkeeper. Several weeks before the dances, a ceremonial committee informally chooses a young boy to be drumkeeper. Being drumkeeper is an expensive honor the boy shares with his family, who must give presents to all the dancers and invited guests. Often families find their budgets severely strained by trying to maintain the level of generosity established by custom. On consecutive weekends, each of the three Osage villages hosts three days of festivities—dancing, eating, and socializing—for the other two villages. Everyone is allowed to dance as long as they are dressed properly— silk shirts, leggings, and imitation roaches for men; silk shawls draped around the shoulders for women. Between the dances, an announcer reads off the gifts as they are presented by the drumkeeper and other members of the tribe wishing to honor the dancers and guests.

The Osage's financial condition has helped the tribe maintain a unique status among American Indians. Living primarily in a state noted for its pan-Indianism—the blending together of tribal cultures into a general "Indian" culture—the Osage have retained their tribal distinctiveness. They stay aloof from most intertribal organizations, and their oil wealth has caused them to be excluded from much legislation designed to benefit American Indians.

Some Osage desire a tribal identity beyond shared ownership in the underground reservation. Attempts have been made to keep the language alive, revive traditional crafts, and preserve ceremonies and rituals. Yet the effects of oil and gas wealth will continue to influence the Osage and other people's perceptions of them.▲

BIBLIOGRAPHY

Bailey, Garrick Alan. *Changes in Osage Social Organization, 1673–1906*. Anthropological Papers no. 5. Eugene: University of Oregon, 1973.

Baird, W. David. *The Osage People*. Phoenix: The Indian Tribal Series, 1972.

Din, Gilbert C., and Abraham P. Nasitir. *The Imperial Osages: Spanish-Indian Diplomacy in the Mississippi Valley*. Norman: University of Oklahoma Press, 1983.

Hodge, Frederick W., ed. *Handbook of American Indians North of Mexico, 1907–1910*. 2 volumes. New York: Rowman, 1975.

LaFlesche, Francis. *Ethnology of the Osage Indian*. Miscellaneous Collection 76. Washington, DC: Smithsonian Institution, 1924.

Mathews, John Joseph. *Osages: Children of the Middle Waters*. Norman: University of Oklahoma Press, 1961.

———. *Wah'Kon-Tah: The Osage and the White Man's Road*. Norman: University of Oklahoma Press, 1932.

The Osages. 5 volumes. New York: Garland American Indian Ethnohistory Series, 1974.

Wilson, Terry P. *Bibliography of the Osage*. Metuchen, NJ: Scarecrow Press, 1985.

———. "Osage Indian Women During a Century of Change, 1870–1980." *Prologue: Journal of the National Archives* 14 (Winter 1982): 185–201.

———. "Osage Oxonian: The Heritage of John Joseph Mathews." *The Chronicles of Oklahoma* 59 (Fall 1981): 264–293.

———. *The Underground Reservation: Osage Oil*. Lincoln: University of Nebraska Press, 1985.

THE OSAGE AT A GLANCE

TRIBE *Osage*

CULTURE AREA *Southern Prairie (Fringe Plains), Central Siouan*

GEOGRAPHY *Before contact: the area that is now Missouri*

Since 1871: northeastern Oklahoma

LINGUISTIC FAMILY *Dhegiha Siouan*

TRADITIONAL ECONOMY *hunting, foraging, horticulture*

FIRST CONTACT *French traders, 1693*

CURRENT POPULATION *10,000 on tribal roll*

FEDERAL STATUS *recognized tribe*

GLOSSARY

allotment U.S. policy, applied nationwide from 1887, to break up tribally owned reservations by assigning individual farms and ranches to Indians. Intended as much to discourage traditional communal activities as to encourage private farming and assimilate Indians into mainstream American life.

allottee The recipient of a share of the tribally owned land and resources of an Indian reservation.

annuities Compensation for land and/or resources, based on terms of treaties or other agreements between the United States and individual tribes; consisted of goods, services, and cash given to the tribe every year for a specified period.

assimilation Adoption by individuals of the customs of another society; a means by which the host society recruits new members. The United States, as well as most American Indian societies, gained new members in this fashion.

band The smallest, simplest type of politically independent society, usually a group of 300 or fewer related persons, which subsists by foraging and occupying a specific territory.

blood quantum Degree of Indian heredity based on the number of a person's ancestors who were Indian. The Osage tribe accepts as members anyone with any Osage ancestry; however, membership in some tribes is defined by a specific minimum of Indian ancestors.

cession A treaty provision whereby a group relinquishes land and property to another group.

civilization program U.S. policy designed to change the Indians' way of life to resemble that of non-Indians; especially focused on getting Indians to adopt Christianity and become farmers.

clan A multigenerational group having a shared identity, organization, and property, based on belief in descent from a common ancestor. Because clan members consider themselves closely related, marriage within the clan is strictly prohibited. Osage clan membership was based on **patrilineal** descent.

competency Legal definition of a person's ability to handle his or her personal and business affairs in the society in which he or she lives. Those judged unable to do so are considered to be incompetent.

coup The highest of all war honors, in which a warrior showed great bravery by touching an enemy with his bare hands or a small stick without killing him. Counting coup is the ceremonial recitation of such acts of bravery in battle.

creation or **origin myth** A sacred narrative that the people of a society believe explains the origins of the world, their own institutions, and their distinctive culture.

culture The knowledge a group has about its world, used to make sense of its experience and as a guide for all its activities.

emigrant Indians Members of tribes originally located in the eastern United States who were forced by the federal government to move west of the Mississippi River.

ga-ni-tha Osage word for the confusion and chaos that existed before the creation of the world.

headright The right of an individual to a full share in the income received communally by an Indian tribe.

hunting-and-gathering; foraging An economic system based on the collection of food by hunting wild animals, fishing, and gathering wild plant foods; the most ancient of human ways of obtaining the necessities of life.

Hunkah Osage word meaning Earth People; one of the two large groups into which the tribe was divided; the division symbolic of war.

Indian Reorganization Act The 1934 federal law that ended the allotment policy and provided for political and economic development of reservation communities.

Little Old Men Council of elder Osage men who set standards of conduct, advised tribal chiefs, and made important decisions governing the tribe.

matrilineal, matrilineality A principle of descent by which kinship is traced through female ancestors; the basis for Osage tribal membership.

Native American Church Of the three North American Indian Peyote religious organizations, the one to which Osage Peyote congregations belong.

pacifist A person who rejects the use of warfare and violence as a means of settling disputes.

patrilineal, patrilineality A principle of descent by which kinship is traced through male ancestors; the basis for Osage divisional and clan membership.

peace-gift A payment of goods to the family of a person killed by a nonfamily member; meant to prevent feuds between families and clans.

peyote A cactus plant native to Texas, New Mexico, Arizona, and the northern Mexican states; used as the vehicle or channel of prayer in the Native American Church.

pipe of peace A sacred pipe symbolic of brotherhood and peace, smoked in turn by those present at special ceremonies to signify adherence to an agreement.

principal chief The leader of the tribe who represents the people when dealing with the outside world, a position instituted by the U.S. government in 1881 to facilitate its treaty negotiations with Indian tribes. In the 20th century, this person is almost always elected by popular vote.

reservation A tract of land set aside by treaty for the occupation and use of Indians; also called a reserve. Some reservations were for entire tribes, many more for individuals and families.

roached hair A hairstyle in which the hair is shaved off close to the scalp on both sides of the head, leaving a ridge, or roach, of hair several inches high down the center of the head.

roadman The person who presides over the prayer meeting in the Native American Church.

royalty A share or percentage of the earnings from the use of a natural resource, in a specified period of time, paid at regular intervals to an owner.

Siouan The related languages spoken by Indians in a large area of the midwestern United States and central Canada. The Osage, Sioux, Iowa, Mandan, Hidatsa, Crow, and Kansa are some Siouan-speaking tribes.

squatters People who occupy land without having legal title to it.

totem An animal or natural object considered to be ancestral to and have special meaning for the people of a given clan; used as a symbol of the clan.

treaty A contract negotiated between representatives of the United States and one or more Indian tribes. Treaties dealt with surrender of political independence, peaceful relations, land sales, boundaries, and related matters.

tribe A type of society consisting of several or many separate communities united by kinship and such social units as clans, religious organizations, economic and political institutions, a common culture, and language. The communities making up a tribe are characterized by economic and political equality and thus lack social classes and authoritative chiefs.

tribal roll A membership list of people considered to belong to a tribe; may include Indian and non-Indian adoptees as well as people received into the tribe through marriage.

Tzi-sho Osage word meaning Sky People; one of the two large groups into which the tribe was divided; the division symbolic of peace.

Wah'Kon-Tah Osage term for the supreme spiritual force in the universe; the creator of the Osage universe.

INDEX

INDEX

Veniard, Etienne, Sieur de
    Bourgmont, 23–24
Verdigris River, 29, 40
Voyageurs, 23

Wah'Kon-tah, 13, 19
Wah-Sha-She, 21
Wah-sho-shah, 95

Wah-ti-an-kah, 53
Walters, Colonel, 63–64,
    73–74
War mourning ceremony,
    34, 99
Washington, George, 26
Watie, Stand, 93
Wheeler-Howard Bill, 88

White Hair. *See* Pawhuska
White Hair, George, 37
Wisconsin River, 21
Women's rights, 95, 97
World War I, 75, 86, 93,
    99
World War II, 93, 101
Wright, J. George, 63, 81

110

PICTURE CREDITS

TERRY P. WILSON is associate professor and coordinator of the Native American studies program and chairman of the department of ethnic studies at the University of California at Berkeley. He was formerly coordinator of Indian culture at Eastern Montana College and professor of history at Southwestern State University in Oklahoma. He holds a B.A. from Phillips University, an M.A. from the University of Oklahoma, and a Ph.D. from Oklahoma State University. He has been coeditor of *The American Indian Quarterly* since 1984 and has published two books and four articles on the Osage.

FRANK W. PORTER III, General Editor of INDIANS OF NORTH AMERICA is Director of the Chelsea House Foundation for American Indian Studies. He holds an M.A. and Ph.D. from the University of Maryland, where he also earned his B.A. He has done extensive research concerning the Indians of Maryland and Delaware and is the author of numerous articles on their history, archaeology, geography, and ethnography. He was formerly Director of the Maryland Commission on Indian Affairs and American Indian Research and Resource Institute, Gettysburg, Pennsylvania, and he has received grants from the Delaware Humanities Forum, the Maryland Committee for the Humanities, the Ford Foundation, and the National Endowment for the Humanities, among others.